CITY FOR CITY

CITY COLLEGE ARCHITECTURAL CENTER
1995 - 2015

207 Street

CITY FOR CITY

CITY COLLEGE ARCHITECTURAL CENTER
1995 - 2015

Text and Introduction by Achva Benzinberg Stein
Preface by Lance Jay Brown

OSCAR RIERA OJEDA
PUBLISHERS

CONTENTS

THE PROJECTS

CHAPTER 01
VISION

CHAPTER 02
EXHIBIT

ACKNOWLEDGMENTS

The generous support of the Rockefeller Brothers Fund has carried the Center for the last decade. Without their continuous advice and financial sustenance the CCAC would not have been able to engage in the projects the center has undertaken. Ben Rodriguez, the Director of the Program at the Rockefeller Brothers Funds has helped the Center in numerous ways. We are deeply indebted to his support and encouragement.

It is important to understand that projects of this type cannot be financed by the community or by municipal agencies. The contributions from foundations such as the Rockefeller Brothers Fund and others, whose names are listed in the acknowledgements, are the "life-line" of any collaboration between educational institutions and community organizations.

I would like to thank Dean Ranalli of the Bernard and Anne Spitzer School of Architecture at CCNY, for helping the previous director and myself to maintain the daily operation of the Center. Dean Ranalli has assisted the Center by allocating (cherished) space, in addition to the communication and IT services. Ranalli also designated funds for the publication of this book.

His belief in the educational value and the benefits of the Center's activities both to the school and the communities has motivated him to continue searching for additional financial support to keep the Center operating in a more stable manner. All those who are involved in the work of the Center appreciate and are indebted to his extensive contribution.

Our thanks also go to all the communities and the residents who partnered with us and who have provided their support and knowledge to the various projects. It is an arduous task for working people to find the time and the strength of motivation to come to meetings. Some such meetings can last long into the night, or are held on the weekend, when these people are needed at home with their families. For all of you and in the name of the past and present CCAC staff, the students, the School and the College, we would like to voice our appreciation and gratitude.

All of us in the Center and in the School are indebted to our wonderful, passionate and hard working students, whose names were not mentioned for lack of space. These many students have joined the center as interns and volunteers. They forge the bond of connection with the communities. Without their devotion to the cause, their resilience, enthusiasm and commitment, no projects or studies would have been able to reach the level which is seen in this book.

Each of the directors, the assistant and the associate directors, whether they served for short or long terms, added stone by stone to the building of the CCAC and to maintaining its mission. Most of the directors have carried the responsibility of managing the Center, in addition to their academic responsibilities, without any or with only very small compensation. Their commitment to creating a bond between "Town and Gown" has been the cornerstone of this work.

The faculty members of the Advisory Board have assisted the Center for many years. The staff and the students have benefited greatly from their contributions. We thank them and the outside members of the Advisory Board for their guidance and their commitment of time and energy.

The list of the consultants is unfortunately incomplete. Many brochures and digital materials were deteriorated or destroyed by viruses and other similar mishaps. Thus the names of some who consulted with us are missing. Whether the names of those individuals appear in the list in this book or not, their help is identified and recognized through the results of the projects the Center has carried out. We thank them and request their forgiveness.

No director can proceed without the help of full time staff. Most of their names appear in the list, however some may have suffered from the same mishaps noted above, and thus their names may not have been included in this publication. I would like to thank them all and let them know that without their dedication and belief in the work of the Center, we would not be able to complete the projects and the book. My personal thanks are specifically directed to Holly Kallman and Rodolfo Leyton who have enthusiastically assisted me and buffered me from many daily difficulties. Rodolfo Leyton has been the person behind collecting, restoring, and enhancing the materials we have used in this publication. This was very tedious work, and I thank him from the bottom of my heart for working under so much stress to bring the book to completion.

Finally but definitely not in order of importance, we would like to thank Ms. Mu'id Niamo Nancy, the Director of Development at The City College of New York. She has been the main force behind the search for financial support in the last ten years. Without her savvy understanding of the development process, the Center would not have been in a position to be granted monetary help. The staff of the Center is grateful for the help they have received from Ms. Regina Masterson, the Research Administrator at The City College of New York. She has chaperoned us through the maze of bureaucracy and made sure that we were able to receive the payments from the agencies which contracted our services.

We are looking forward to another decade of collaborative work and stimulating learning experiences.

Achva Benzinberg Stein, FASLA
Professor and Director
City College Architectural Center
Landscape Architecture Graduate Program
Bernard and Anne Spitzer School of Architecture
City College Of New York

PREFACE

The City College Architectural Center owes much to both the community it serves and the community that has served it, from citizen clients to directors, advisors, faculty, architects, educators, student interns, community activists, foundations, and government officials. The community served has generously welcomed our students and taught them the value of social engagement and social responsibility and the City College and the School of Architecture with its architecture, urban design, and landscape architecture expertise and creativity has enriched the lives of those benefiting from its collaboration. The CCAC is people.

City for City has been a long time in the making, over 30 years. It is a step on the ladder of democracy that was affirmed and reaffirmed after the tumultuous years of the 1960s. While this publication highlights the more recent activities of the City College Architectural Center it stands on the shoulders of a movement that resulted in the creation of over 100 community design centers nationwide. These centers were, and still are, a model for service, learning, for working both with and for "not-for-profit, community organizations concerned with the physical and economic development of their neighborhoods."

Each of the projects documented is the result of a commitment to a set of values that has expanded and become more explicit over the passing years. First and foremost is a sense of equity and social justice. Technical assistance and advocacy in planning and design were among the earliest services offered by the CCAC. Initially, working in a district as socially diverse as that of Northern Manhattan paved the way for social discourse so necessary to participatory decision-making. By engaging the various disciplines of the school and the college the CCAC seeks to advance the right of every person to live in an economically and environmentally healthy neighborhood, district, and region. In seeking to support these values the Center pursues research, education, and best practices that lead to place-based design excellence through collaborative and integrated processes.

From its inception the CCAC has been committed to improving the urban environment and the complementary natural features. The Center recognizes the ever shifting needs of our evolving demographics and works to mediate and collaborate as needed and required by local circumstances while maintaining an abiding commitment to design excellence.

In the words of the Ephebic Oath recited by all graduates of The City College of New York and embodied in the mission of the CCAC, "We will strive to transmit this city not only not less, but greater, better, and more beautiful than it was transmitted to us."

Lance Jay Brown, FAIA
ACSA Distinguished Professor
New York, May 2010

INTRODUCTION

The City College Architectural Center, a research center housed within City College's Bernard and Anne Spitzer School of Architecture, was founded more than thirty years ago by a group of civic-minded designers determined to use the resources of the school to work for the social, physical, and economic improvement of New York City and its surroundings. The center offers technical assistance and advocacy support to not-for-profit community organizations engaged in improving the quality of life for city residents. It also conducts research on issues pertaining to the urban environment, using its academic expertise to help build real-world solutions to the city's problems.

As a community design center, the CCAC's mission is to directly engage with local community stakeholders to improve the quality of the built and natural environment. All of the participants benefit from the CCAC's work: communities receive technical expertise, grant-writing assistance, and professional design advice they could not otherwise afford; students have the opportunity to engage in real-world learning exercises and develop a greater awareness of their social responsibility as designers; and faculty members are able to continue with meaningful professional work as they educate the next generation of designers in their role as stewards of the city. The city benefits as well from design solutions that blend the experiential knowledge of community members with the professional expertise of the CCAC faculty, staff, and students.

The CCAC had its genesis in the community design movement of the 1960s, which aimed to make cities' bureaucratic planning processes more open, inclusive, and responsive to community needs and wishes. The community design process strives to include all stakeholder voices in an equitable and open dialogue to improve the environment for the broad range of community residents.

It is the role of the community design center to act as an advocate for communities with limited capacity to plan for or implement much-needed physical changes to their neighborhoods. Traditionally, community design centers have seen it as their mission to act as a counterbalance to the prevailing weight of government and developer interests and to advocate for solutions that represent the interests of local low and moderate income residents as well. Community design centers also serve as training resources that help community leaders learn how to advocate successfully with local governments, fund important neighborhood projects, and become empowered participants in the processes that determine their community's future.

The CCAC is a proud participant in this tradition of civic advocacy and social justice. Many of the projects highlighted in this book involve historically underserved neighborhoods and groups in the New York metropolitan area. CCAC professionals and students have produced educational materials documenting environmental justice issues in upper Manhattan and walking tour maps to the architectural heritage of Harlem; assisted a local youth group in developing its vision for converting a disused Bronx library building into a community center; produced an exhibit of design changes that would transform the Amsterdam Avenue streetscape in Harlem; conducted planning studies in how to capitalize on the heritage of Northern Manhattan and identify priority issues in the development of the Washington Heights and Inwood neighborhoods; and created a community centered counterproposal to DOT improvements scheduled for Malcolm X Boulevard. The center created a comprehensive redevelopment plan for the City of Mount Vernon and for 106th Street in Manhattan; a gateway plan for the Village of Hempstead; and an urban design study of the Bradhurst neighborhood in Harlem. The CCAC has also produced designs for the renovation of a community center and children's park in the Bronx and a plaza at Amsterdam Avenue and 146th Street, among others.

The CCAC's importance to the community and fulfillment of its mission can be read in this record of successful civic engagement and advocacy. But the twenty-first century has brought new challenges and reveals some of the conflicts inherent in the conceptual model of community design centers in general. Among the issues is the difficult relationship between "town and gown." The educational institutions that house these centers have strong connections to federal and state agencies and are often financially supported by the local governments. This special position places the university outside the boundaries of the community regardless of its physical location. Furthermore, few if any of the faculty members live in the neighborhood where the projects are being undertaken. They usually come from different economic backgrounds than local residents, and even if some of them were raised in the same area where the university is located, their connections have been lost.

Universities that sponsor community design centers also require that the results of the work of these centers be published and recorded as educational or professional experience within a short time of their completion. Truly effective community assistance typically takes a very long time to mature and produce results. Creating trust between neighborhoods and "outsider" professionals and students requires building relationships over time, which is difficult to accomplish under these circumstances, especially because of the high turnover in student involvement and the pressure on faculty members to constantly find new projects for their latest classes.

Student interns and the faculty members who supervise them live by academic schedules, which come in sixteen-week blocks. But often, a project can only be completed well after the students have left for vacation or even after they have graduated, leaving the faculty members who assisted with and supervised their work responsible for finishing and delivering the project. This work is voluntary and is neither financially compensated nor does it count toward academic advancement. This poses an additional burden on junior faculty members who must focus their efforts on obtaining tenure, because community design work takes time away from research or undertaking design projects in their professional practices, the two generally accepted paths toward academic advancement. Finally, a change of faculty assignments or a change of place makes it difficult to establish strong connections with the community, creating a trust vacuum that requires time for new personnel to build new connections.

The financial burden on community design centers is enormous. Traditionally, they have relied for funding on the community groups who approach them to help them find solutions to specific problems they have identified. While much valuable work has come from this approach, successful projects need stable, extended sources of funding, and most community groups are not equipped to be long-term fundraising channels. Public universities also suffer from precarious funding situations, and funds can be reduced or stopped altogether any time there is a change in administrative priorities. Nor are foundations a reliable source of ongoing funding. They tend to change their priorities and many also limit their contributions to project expenses only and are unwilling to cover the overhead cost of running a professional design center. Today, private universities are the institutions most likely to succeed in providing long-term assistance to communities, thanks to their large endowments and their ability to raise outside funds.

Community design centers face challenges that go beyond funding. Over the past 20 years, the idea of community design has shifted from placing value on community participation to an emphasis on physical design to solve community issues. Community development has been required to increasingly focus on project economics, with the result that community building often takes a lower priority in the development process.

In practice, we now see that communities are often presented with solutions to approve, rather than being invited to participate in a genuinely collaborative effort to develop those solutions. Often, community groups lack the experience or expertise to identify potential problems or evaluate planned development scenarios that would negatively impact their neighborhoods.

While the tremendous increase of community-based organizations over the last twenty years has partially fulfilled the hopes of professionals who were involved in such work in the 1960s, continued progress requires a response to the new challenges that communities face. It is now time for community design centers to rethink their traditional activism. The CCAC and other community design centers could use their expertise and manpower proactively, acting as watchdogs for the community by alerting local groups to issues that will affect their neighborhoods in time for those groups to participate constructively in finding equitable solutions. Such a shift would also bring community design centers opportunities for research, study and evaluation of projects.

In the new model of the community design center, professional activism would be supported and enriched by the research capabilities of the university. Today, we recognize the importance of seeking sustainable ways to grow and develop; such solutions can only be achieved with the input of many professionals working as a team. This new sustainability paradigm has increased the opportunities for professionals from a wide range of university disciplines to engage in local community development projects exponentially. Together, university experts could work to develop, research, and test new models for community-based design, greatly benefiting real-world commercial institutions such as developers and lenders by offering them successful community participation models that produce solid results and ensure the engagement of local citizens and their support for the cooperatively developed design solutions.

The missing key to the growth and adaptation of the community design centers is revamping the ways in which they are funded. By making the commitment to providing long-term, stable funding, foundation and grant producing agencies could significantly increase the effectiveness of each dollar they spend.

The new model of an activist, research-based, consistently funded community design center would help provide local citizens with a real, effective voice in the development of their communities. At the same time, the new model would enhance the mission of centers like the CCAC by benefiting the communities, the city, the university, and the educational process as well.

The CCAC stands ready to move into the twenty-first century, built on a solid background of achievement, a dedicated faculty and students enthusiastic about testing their knowledge and skills in the evolving world of design and community development.

Achva Benzinberg Stein, FASLA
Professor and Director
City College Architectural Center
Landscape Architecture Graduate Program
Bernard and Anne Spitzer School of Architecture
City College Of New York

THE PROJECTS

CHAPTER 01

VISION

ENVIRONMENTAL JUSTICE
SEMINAR & BOOKLET

CHAPTER 01

PARTNERS:

Van Alen Institute.
Graham Foundation.
Ursula Warchol, Weisz and Warchol Studio.

DATE OF PROJECT:

1996

This pamphlet resulted from a sponsored seminar conducted at the City College School of Architecture in the spring of 1996. The seminar was developed to provide an opportunity to establish a linkage between design education and the environmental realties of inner-city communities. Community activists and design professionals participated in panel discussions and community reviews.

The Environmental Justice seminar was supported by a grant from the Van Alen Institute's Projects in Public Architecture program. The exhibit and accompanying pamphlet, designed by Ursula Warchol of the Weisz and Warchol Studio, were developed with the support of a grant from the Graham Foundation.

The pamphlet records the students' efforts to document four selected environmental justice issues: (1) reinterpreting public places, (2) accessing cyberspace, (3) defining spatial ownership, and (4) creating history in a creative and community-friendly way. It includes a collection of essays, maps, and student work focussed on achieving environmental justice in the Hamilton Heights and Manhattanville neighborhoods of New York City.

ENVIRONMENTAL JUSTICE

Solutions for the Inner City

ENVIRONMENTAL JUSTICE

PROGRESS
NATURE
MANMADE
SHELTER
ECOLOGY
REFUGE
JUNCTION
PEOPLE

The movement for environmental justice condemns the fact that a disproportionate burden of environmental harm is borne by communities of color, and seeks to equitably distribute the benefits of environmental protection.

The isolation of stigmatized facilities from the financial and political centers of the city occurs at the cost of entire neighborhoods, which are often already disadvantaged by a lack of economic stability and political influence. This isolation, however, is only virtual; indeed, the revelation of the cumulative human and economic consequences of discriminatory site selection have renewed the debate on the ecosystemic nature of cities. A neighborhood plagued with higher levels of air pollution, chronic asthma among its population, and foul smelling air will also suffer from depressed real estate values and economic stagnation; but doesn't the city as a whole suffer from the existence of such pockets of depression, whether it be ethically, economically, or politically? By virtue of its density and political unity, a city cannot afford to be at odds with its own organs. Despite the fact that distinct social communities may coexist in a city, the city remains a biological whole.

Environmental Justice therefore implies a re-evaluation of the relationship between specific sites, social / racial / financial communities, and the urban fabric. The most difficult challenges faced by the movement at present are the improvement of community access to environmental and political information, and the linkage of various community-based environmental struggles.

Next page. Pamphlet, *Environmental Justice is...*

Environmental justice is...

PROGRESS NATURE MANMADE SHELTER

ECOLOGY REFUGE JUNCTION PEOPLE

en·vi·ron·men·tal (ĕn-vī'rən-mĕn'tl, -vī'ar... relating to, or associated with the environment. 2 being concerned with the ecological impact of alt... ronment. 3. Medicine. Of or relating to potential... tors originating in the environment: environmental... vi'ron·men'tal·ly adv.

jus·tice (jŭs'tĭs) n. 1. The quality of being just... The principle of moral rightness; equity. b. Conf... rightness in action or attitude; righteousness. 3. ... ing of what is just, especially fair treatment and... accordance with honor, standards, or law. b. Le... istration and procedure of law. 4. Conformity t... sound reason: *The overcharged customer was angr...* tice. 5. *Abbr.* J., J. Law. a. A judge. b. A justi... —*idiom.* **do justice to.** To treat adequately, fair... appreciation: *The subject is so complex that I cann...*

Environmental justice means having laws to govern planning and zoning issues in the fields of architecture and urban planning. I see this course as related to law, and the status of an architect being that of a judge. An architect interprets laws that shape our city, streets, and buildings, the same way a judge interprets the laws written by legislative branch to govern and set the moral standards by which we live. When our codes and zoning resolutions are well written our communities can become a pleasant place for living, studying, and working. (left) A housing project that seems welcoming inviting, safe, and engages the greenery.

Sometimes when more green is added to a city or urban planning project it does not mean that the project is going to work. In New York City, for example, public housing was thought to be the solution for green architecture. Stacking housing in towers to create open land and plazas at grade. As a social experiment this did not work. (right) A setting illustrating how nature has been considered by the indigeneous societies of Japan. The architecture becomes organic, natural, an oasis.

Nuclear power plants, Oil refineries, and dams are needed to create a source of power to fuel cars, heat and cool homes, businesses and schools. The byproducts of this industrial development are polluting our natural and man made environments. Our drinking water, air, and farming grounds are being affected. Regardless of alternate waste management, human beings have not created a foolproof waste treatment system. There is an abundance of technologies on the market but only a society with the means can afford to have these systems. For now we can all recycle and save our trees and supply of iron ore.

-John Alvarado

The concept of Environmental Justice is one that I can not easily explain. I can begin by saying that what it is not is the placement of a structure or object on an area that would have a negative impact on the environment and/or the people who have to live around it. As an architect, I view Environmental Justice as being sensitive to the needs of the people and surroundings. It is a concept that should always be present in our thoughts from the initial stages of our design process. I have chosen simple words to describe a concept that is not so simple, but should be much more common to the practice of architecture.

-Reinaldo Garcia

ENVIRONMENTAL JUSTICE HAS TWO ISSUES:

- THE PROTECTION, PRESERVATION AND CARE OF OUR NATURAL RESOURCES FROM HUMAN CONTAMINATION CAUSING SUCH ILLS AS THE DESTRUCTION OF WATER AND THE ECOSYSTEM
- THE ACTUAL COMMUNITIES THAT ARE DIRECTLY AFFECTED WHO ARE AT TIMES THE PEOPLE OF COLOR, AND OTHER SEGMENTS OF THE POPULATION WHO ARE OFTEN POWERLESS TO ORGANIZE IN THEIR BEST INTERESTS....

-JOEL RIVERA

REINTERPRETATION OF PUBLIC PLACES

The alterations of public open space are minimized and aligned closer to community needs when the designer, planner, public official and others respond to the multiple layers of community space needs and methods of establishing the neighborhood social value placed on those spaces.

> In all these ways, the most public of spaces have been the least amenable to continuous control, although control may be harshly exerted when the dominant interests of society are contested in those spaces...
>
> - Karen A. Frank,
> **Ordinary Space**

Next page. Pamphlet, *Public Places*

Reinterpretation of Public Places

The alterations to public open space are minimized and aligned closer to community needs when the designer, planner, public official and others respond to the multiple layers of community space needs and and methods of establishing the neighborhood social value placed on those spaces.

In all these ways, the most public of spaces have been the least amenible to continuous control, although control may be harshly exerted when the dominant interests of society are contested in those spaces...

–Karen A. Franck, *Ordinary Space*

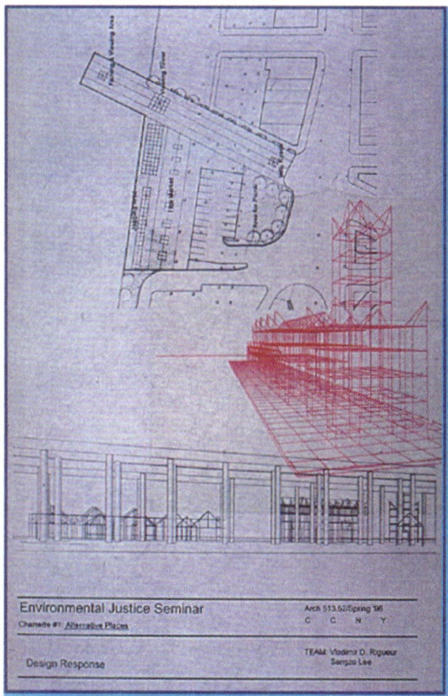

This seminar project challenged students to move through the Hamilton Heights/Manhattanville community in search of places that had a clear program of use that dictated its physical structure and use patterns, yet were utilized differently than planned. Opportunities were identified and methods established for enhancing the residents' use of and perception of public open spaces in their community. Through interviews with residents, visual observation of neighborhood and photographic recording, students took the traditional design process steps of inventory and analysis, beyond the aesthetic into the realm of cultural appropriateness.

The reinterpretation of space by users is universal. However, this reinterpretation of space use and the social value placed on those spaces is particularily prevalent within communities with a history of economic, social, political and environmental disenfranchisement. The shift in public open space uses and open space value within the Hamilton Heights/Manhattanville neighborhood in Harlem is driven by its ethnic diversity and physical location.

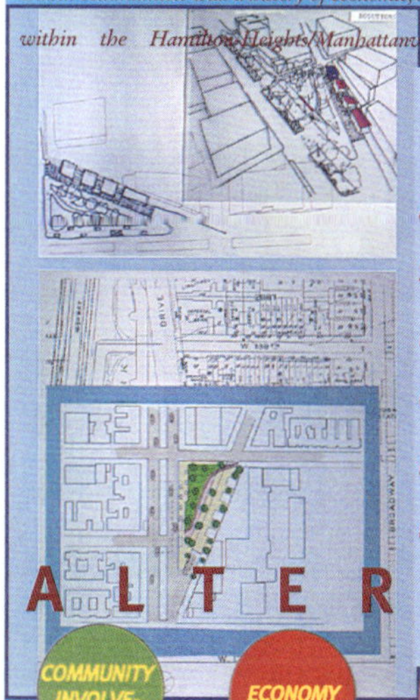

INTENDED USE versus ACTUAL USE

Streets used as play areas:
Parking lots as markets:
Gardens in vacant housing lots:
Passive activities in traffic medians.

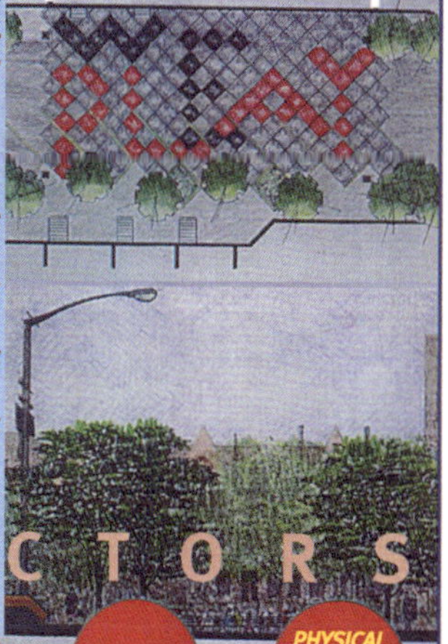

ALTERING FACTORS

COMMUNITY INVOLVEMENT · ECONOMY · ETHNIC DIVERSITY · GEOGRAPHY · SHIFTING PUBLIC FUNDING · IMMIGRATION · PHYSICAL ENVIRONMENT

ACCESSING CYBERSPACE

How is the Information Superhighway best accessed in ethnically diverse communities to action equity and power?
How can an information network be localized within a community yet linked to the centers of finance?
How can sites within a community join to provide access to information, creating known places of economic power?

Modern communications technologies have expanded awareness of our shared dependence on one fragile planetary ecosystem and the universality of the failure of the mega institutions that govern the planet.

- David C. Karten

Next page. Pamphlet, *Accessing Cyberspace*

Accessing Cyberspace

How is the Information Superhighway best accessed in ethnically diverse communities to attain equity and power?

How can an information network be localized within a community yet linked to the centers of finance?

How can sites within a community join with access to information, creating known places of economic power?

Modern communications technologies have expanded awareness of our shared dependence on one fragile planetary ecosystem and the universality of the failure of the mega institutions that govern the planet.

-David C. Korten,
Toward Sustainable Livelihood

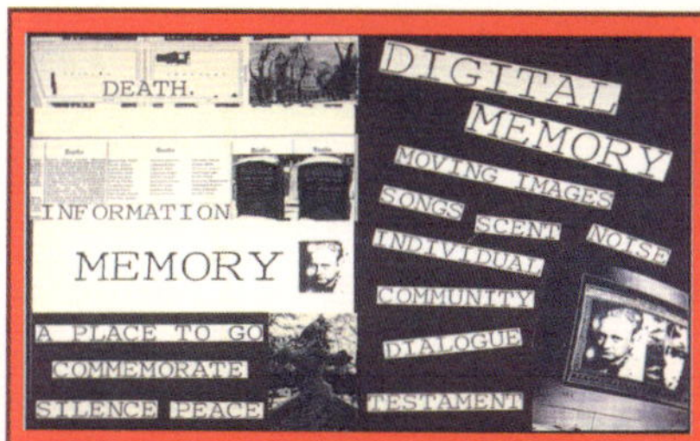

In an era of corporate downsizing, governmental budget cuts, privatization of public facilities, and cuts in social services, economically stressed communities must explore alternate methods of accessing the financial power bases outside and within the community. Cyberspace, Internet and the Superhighway provide the contemporary access roadmap to economic empowerment within historically disenfranchised communities.

Students explored the potential for creating information access places that would become economic, public service, and political vehicles to community power. Students established theoretical scenerios for creating economic development opportunities within the Hamilton-Heights/Manhattanville community by exploring places of public value. Parks: churches: schools: banks: commercial space: government centers: transportation nodes: and residential spaces form a partial list of possible locations for informational access places within the community. The identification of a public open space / cyberspace network of community places provides opportunities for communities to increase the value of public open space as well as sustain spaces economically for the benefit of an entire community.

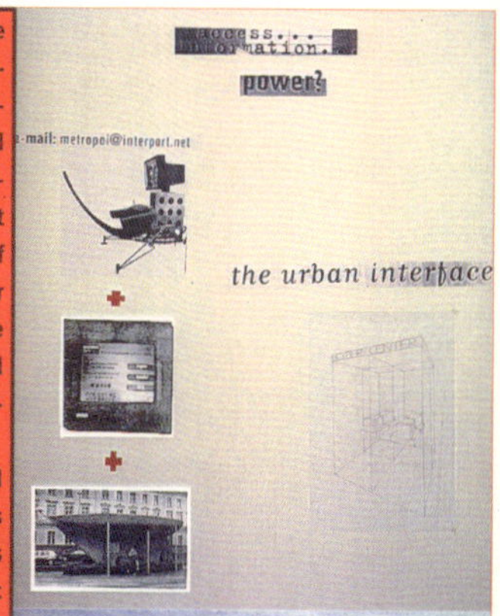

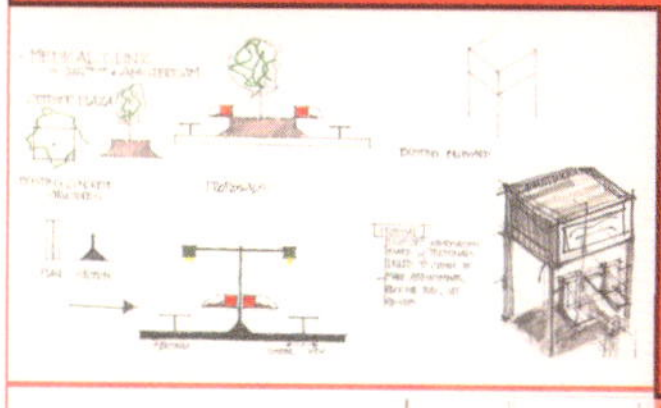

GIVEN THE OPPORTUNITIES OPENED BY THE ELECTRONIC REVOLUTION AND DRIVEN BY COMPUTER TECHNOLOGIES, HOW CAN A COMMUNITY, THROUGH PUBLIC OPEN SPACE, ACCESS ECONOMIC INFORMATION THAT WILL BENEFIT AN ENTIRE COMMUNITY? THIS PIVOTAL QUESTION FORMED THE BASIS OF THIS SEMINAR PROJECT AND ITS RELATIONSHIP TO PUBLIC OPEN SPACE ISSUES.

REDEFINING SPATIAL OWNERSHIP

What design steps can be taken to turn public housing into an "urban home"?
Can Design reconcile housing towers with the neighborhood and street grid?
How can the physical nature of this community be understood and protected?

People have affirmed their cultural identity... to restore whatever limited control they can over work and residence, to reinvent love and laughter in the midst of the abstraction of the new historical landscape...

- Manuel Castello,
The City

Next page. Pamphlet, *Redefining Spatial Ownership*

Redefining Spatial Ownership

- What design steps can be taken to turn public housing into an "urban home"?
- Can design reconcile the housing towers with the neighborhood and street grid?
- How can the physical nature of this community be understood and protected?

People have affirmed their cultural identity...to restore whatever limited control they can over work and residence, to reinvent love and laughter in the midst of the new historical landscape...

- Manuel Castells,
The Informational City

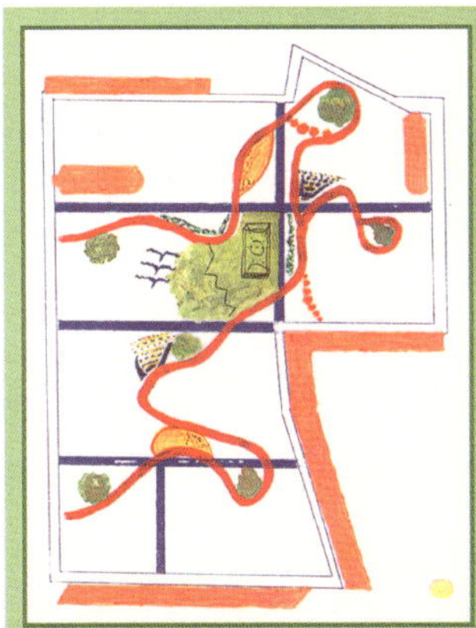

Barriers, physical in nature, often extend into the realm of the perceptual. These are implied through social or cultural activity within a given space. How the public, semi-public and private spaces and the transtional spaces that divide them are articulated; and how a community can become involved in defining public open space and solving the barriers that often blur the physical boundaries of community space; these are the major questions explored within this seminar project.

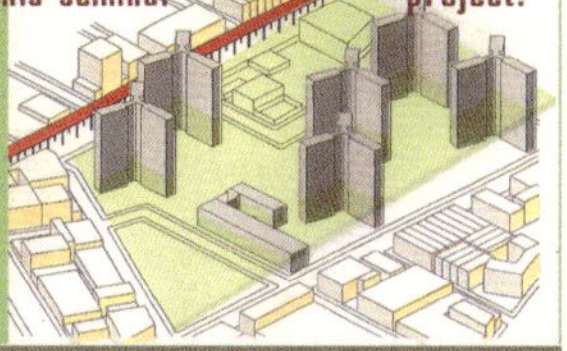

Public open space must exist without barriers, forming a sense of collective community ownership. When there is spatial ambiguity within a community, public open space is set adrift - underutilized or abandoned. Thus it is crucial to clarify the spatial zones of ownership and use, breaking down the barriers and boundaries that render such spaces useless.

UTILIZING PUBLIC HOUSING SPACE FACTORS, STUDENTS EXAMINED THE POTENTIAL FOR CLOSER PHYSICAL AND PERCEPTUAL RELATIONSHIPS BETWEEN THE DOMINANT GRIDDED SYSTEM OF THE HAMILTON-HEIGHTS / MANHATTANVILLE COMMUNITY AND THE GEOMETRICALLY DIVERSE PUBLIC HOUSING DEVELOPMENTS. THIS JUXTAPOSITION WAS VIEWED AS A METHOD OF ENHANCING SPATIAL UNITY AND FORMING COHERENT ROADMAP TOWARD A NETWORK OF OPEN SPACES WITHIN THE COMMUNITY.

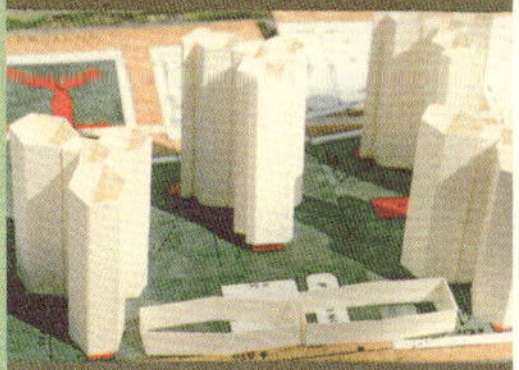

Public housing was utilized as a vehicle for examining these issues and adapting public open space for maximum community use.

CREATING HISTORY

Can preservation define guidelines of future designs, and, rather than mimic the past, can it be the bridge between the past and the present?
Can preservation become the anchor of development and spearhead changes? As it reaches to the roots of a community, can it become the tool of its transformation? How can "cultural preservation" act to expand the scale and types of places to be preserved in a community, enhancing and celebrating its cultural diversity?

> The preservation of the collective memory through the preservation of physical places is a fundamental need today for a society determined not to give up its power to build.
>
> - Gae Aulenti

Next page. Pamphlet, *Creating History*

Creating History

- Can preservation define guidelines of future designs, and, rather than mimic the past, can it be the bridge between the past and the present?

- Can preservation become the anchor of development and spearhead changes? As it reaches to the roots of a community, can it become the tool of its transformation?

- How can 'cultural preservation' act to expand the scale and types of places to be preserved in a community, enhancing and celebrating its cultural diversity?

The preservation of a collective memory through the preservation of physical places is a fundamental need today for a society determined not to give up its power to build...

-Gae Aulenti,
in an interview 8/96

he proposed relocation of Alexander Hamilton's Grange into nearby Saint Nicholas Park, was an oppurunity to make the past more visible, while re-creating the 'flavor' of the Grange's original setting, nd strengthening other redevelopment projects within the immediate area. The relocation of the Grange does not involve any demolition, and the borrowing of park land to site it was acceptable only to the degree that it enhanced the public quality and use of Saint Nicholas Park.

A NEIGHBORHOOD CAN BE INTERPRETED AS THE PHYSICAL EXPRESSION OF A COMMUNITY'S **COLLECTIVE MEMORY.** FROM THIS PERSPECTIVE, PUBLIC AND OPEN SPACES ARE OPPORTUNITIES TO EITHER READ OR TELL THE STORY OF THAT COMMUNITY. IN NEIGHBORHOODS IN TRANSITION, WHERE CULTURAL. SOCIAL, AND EVEN ECONOMIC CONDITIONS ARE CHANGING, THERE IS A NEED TO IDENTIFY WAYS OF MAKING THE COMMMUNITY'S PAST HISTORY COME TO LIFE IN A MEANINGFUL WAY AS WELL AS CREATING SPATIAL ELEMENTS THAT WILL SERVE AS FUTURE HISTORICAL LANDMARKS, TO CELEBRATE THE NEIGHBORHOOD'S DIVERSITY AND ITS MEANING WITH RESPECT TO THE LARGER CITY.

ENVIRONMENTAL JUSTICE WILL BE ACHIEVED WHEN PROPOSED PRESERVATION INTERVENTIONS WILL KNIT THE OLD AND THE NEW INTO AN URBAN FABRIC RECONCILING THE PRESSURES OF THE PAST WITH THE NEEDS OF THE FUTURE.

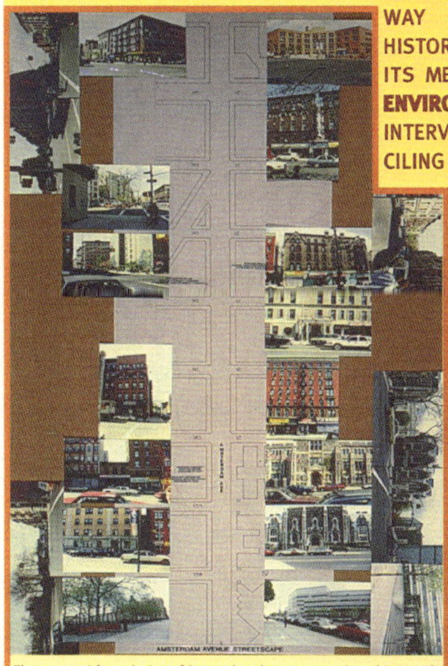

The proposal for redesign of Amsterdam Avenue recognizes this stretch of the avenue as it marks the cultural boundary between predominantly black and predominantly Latino neighborhoods. If historic references can give the street unity, the recognition of new cultural influences, through secondary design features was seen as important.

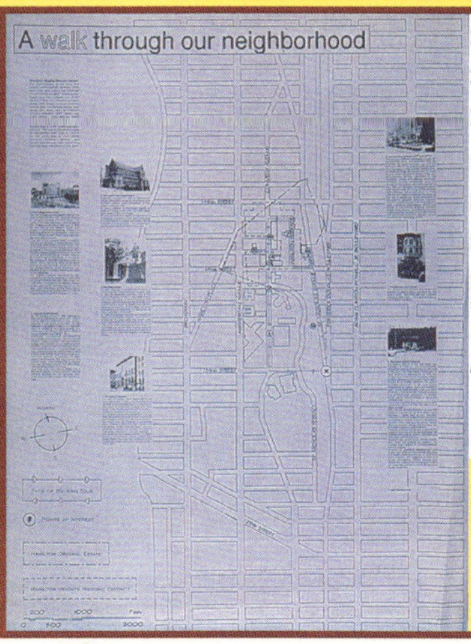

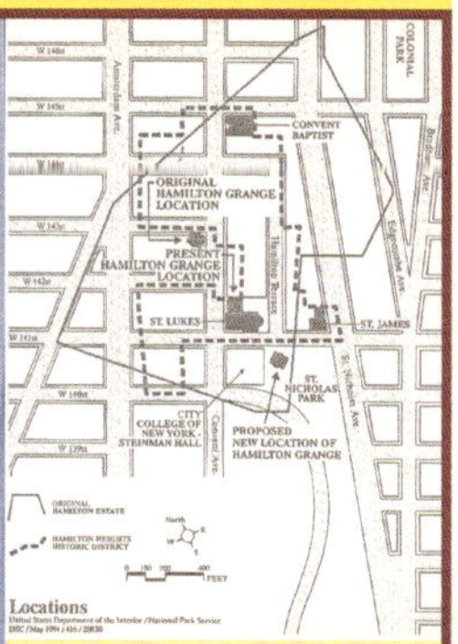

This walking tour map of the Hamilton Heights Historic District attempts to interpret the recent socio-cultural history of the neighborhood by focusing on historical markers which highlight the cultural diversity of the community and uses the walking tour as a means to weave issues, controversies, community achieve-ments and proposals into a counterpoint to traditional designs.

WALKING TOUR MAPS OF HARLEM

CHAPTER 01

PARTNERS:

Office of Manhattan Borough President Ruth W. Messinger.
Architecture, Planning and Design Program of the New York State Council on the Arts.
Upper Manhattan Empowerment Zone Development.

CORPORATION:

Tourism Grant Program, City of New York.
Consolidated Edison.

DATE OF PROJECT:

1999

The CCAC researched and designed two walking tour maps of historic Harlem in northern Manhattan, one exploring its landmarks, the other its residential districts, with the intention of familiarizing students with the area surrounding City College, exploring the neighborhood's cultural legacy, and helping to promote tourism in the area.

Originally Nieuw Haarlem, a Dutch farming settlement founded in 1658, the area remained rural well into the mid-nineteenth century. Harlem urbanized rapidly with the arrival of the elevated trains in the 1880s, eventually expanding to include the area between 110th and 155th streets. Around the turn of the twentieth century, African-American New Yorkers started moving uptown into Harlem's new apartment buildings and town houses, drawn by the plentiful housing supply, cheap rents, and the promotional efforts of African-American real estate entrepreneurs. By the time of Harlem's golden era in the 1920s, it had become the most famous black community in the United States.

Today, after a period of economic decline, the area is seeing new families move into its restored brownstone and limestone buildings. The combination of architectural treasures and unique cultural institutions—including music venues, restaurants, and museums—make Harlem a destination for New Yorkers and tourists alike. The map Landmarks of Harlem is one of the CCAC's most popular products, providing a detailed foldout plan of the area complete with photos and a suggested walking tour highlighting Harlem's social and architectural history.

The CCAC compiled a separate map of Harlem's residential districts, At Home in Harlem. In the early twentieth century, residential neighborhoods like Sugar Hill were popular with prominent African Americans, including W. E. B. Du Bois, Thurgood Marshall, Langston Hughes, Adam Clayton Powell Jr., Zora Neale Hurston, and Duke Ellington and were at the center of the Harlem Renaissance. Sugar Hill's historical significance has been recognized by the New York City Landmarks Preservation Commission, and it is listed on the U.S. National Register of Historic Places.

LANDMARKS OF HARLEM

LANDMARKS OF HARLEM

AN ARCHITECTURAL WALKING TOUR

The Great Black Way

Cultural Center of Harlem

Sugar Hill District

Morningside Heights

Central & East Harlem

Hamilton Heights

Other Points of Interest

Top. Landmarks of Harlem

Next page. Landmarks of Harlem, an architectural walking tour

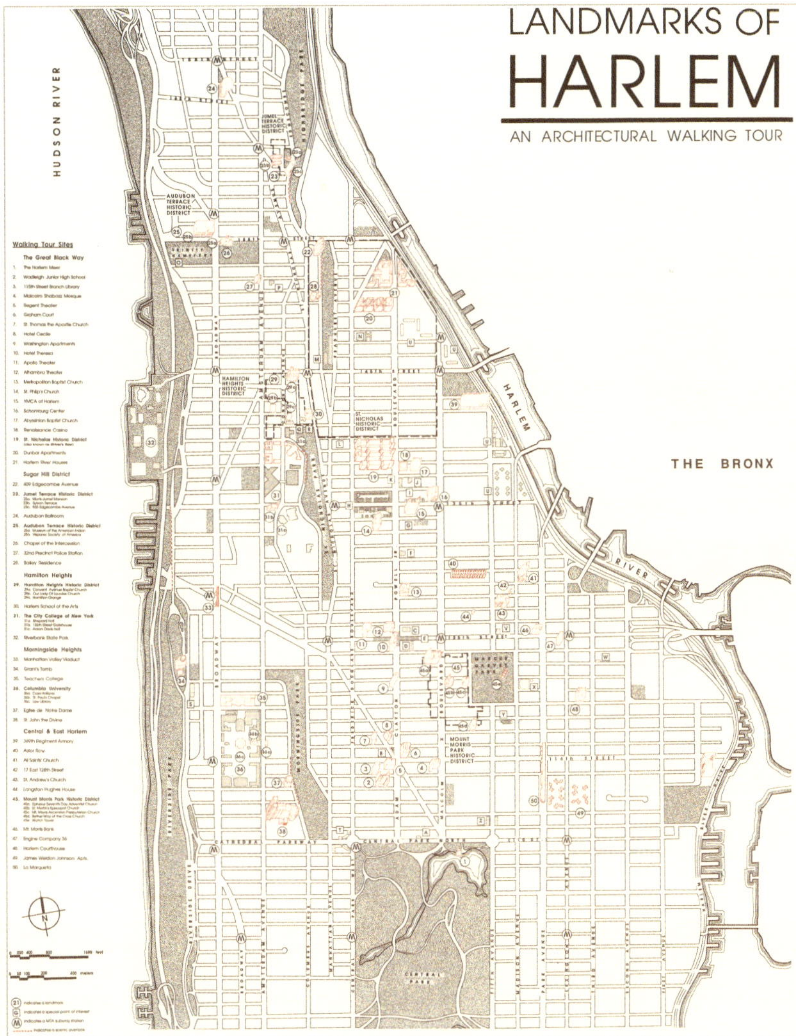
LANDMARKS OF
HARLEM
AN ARCHITECTURAL WALKING TOUR
HUDSON RIVER
THE BRONX
HARLEM RIVER
HAMILTON HEIGHTS HISTORIC DISTRICT
ST. NICHOLAS HISTORIC DISTRICT
AUDUBON TERRACE HISTORIC DISTRICT
JUMEL TERRACE HISTORIC DISTRICT
MOUNT MORRIS PARK HISTORIC DISTRICT
CENTRAL PARK
Walking Tour Sites
The Great Black Way
1. The Harlem Meer
2. Wadleigh Junior High School
3. 115th Street Branch Library
4. Malcolm Shabazz Mosque
5. Regent Theater
6. Graham Court
7. St. Thomas the Apostle Church
8. Hotel Cecile
9. Washington Apartments
10. Hotel Theresa
11. Apollo Theater
12. Alhambra Theater
13. Metropolitan Baptist Church
14. St. Philip's Church
15. YMCA of Harlem
16. Schomburg Center
17. Abyssinian Baptist Church
18. Renaissance Casino
19. St. Nicholas Historic District
20. Dunbar Apartments
21. Harlem River Houses
Sugar Hill District
22. 409 Edgecombe Avenue
23. Jumel Terrace Historic District
24. Audubon Ballroom
25. Audubon Terrace Historic District
26. Chapel of the Intercession
27. 32nd Precinct Police Station
28. Bailey Residence
Hamilton Heights
29. Hamilton Heights Historic District
30. Harlem School of the Arts
31. The City College of New York
32. Riverbank State Park
Morningside Heights
33. Manhattan Valley Viaduct
34. Grant's Tomb
35. Teachers College
36. Columbia University
37. Eglise de Notre Dame
38. St. John the Divine
Central & East Harlem
39. 369th Regiment Armory
40. Astor Row
41. All Saints' Church
42. 17 East 128th Street
43. St. Andrew's Church
44. Langston Hughes House
45. Mount Morris Park Historic District
46. Mt. Morris Bank
47. Engine Company 36
48. Harlem Courthouse
49. James Weldon Johnson Apts.
50. La Marqueta
N

Top. At Home in Harlem

Next page. At Home in Harlem, an architectural walking tour

AT HOME IN
HARLEM
AN ARCHITECTURAL WALKING TOUR
HUDSON RIVER
THE BRONX
HARLEM RIVER
Tour Sites
1. West 135th Street Apartments
2. Lenox Terrace
3. Striver's Row (St. Nicholas Historic District)
4. Dunbar Apartments
5. Harlem River Houses
6. Esplanade Gardens
7. Polo Grounds Towers
8. 409 Edgecombe Avenue
9. 555 Edgecombe Avenue
10. Jumel Terrace Historic District
11. Morris-Jumel Mansion
12. Sylvan Terrace
13. Duke Ellington Residence
14. The Grinnell
15. Yellow Clapboard Villa
16. Bailey Residence
17. Lower Edgecombe Avenue
18. Riverbend
19. Riverton
20. Astor Row
21. Langston Hughes Residence
22. Mount Morris Park Historic District
23. Victorian Row
24. Taino Towers
25. 1199 Plaza
26. The Project Wall
27. General Atlantic Houses
28. Arthur A. Schomburg Plaza
29. The Semiramis
30. West 114th Street
31. Graham Court
32. Hotel Cecile
33. Washington Apartments
34. Hotel Theresa
35. St. Nicholas Houses
36. Lionel Hampton Houses
37. Minnie L. Wilson Towers
38. Towers on the Park
39. Manhattan Valley Townhouses
40. Cathedral Parkway
41. Morningside Gardens
42. Ulysses S. Grant Houses
43. 41 Convent Avenue
44. Hamilton Heights Historic District
45. Hamilton Grange
46. 19 Hamilton Terrace
N

VILLAGE OF HEMPSTEAD GATEWAY

CHAPTER 01

PARTNERS:

Village of Hempstead.
Village of Hempstead Community Development Agency.
State of New York Division of Coastal Resources.

DATE OF PROJECT:

2006 - 2009

The Village of Hempstead contracted with the CCAC to undertake the design of the Peninsula Boulevard entrance to the village. Although it is the gateway to the town, there is no clear marker for this entrance. There are also traffic issues at this site, since Peninsula Boulevard serves as a major commuter artery from Long Island into New York City in the morning and in the opposite direction in the late afternoon. This period of heavy traffic coincides with students coming and going from the nearby high school. The combination of a lack of appropriate signage and heavy traffic creates a very hazardous situation for pedestrians.

The CCAC provided alternative traffic and visual solutions to the design of the boulevard and suggested the creation of a rotary to mark the point of entry gateway and at the same time reduce the danger from traffic.

In addition, the CCAC delineated a "safe route to school" along the reconstructed Horse Creek and proposed solving the highway drainage problem by constructing a wetland on the school property that could also serve as an outdoor classroom. The CCAC suggested an alternative design for the high school campus, including provision of an inflatable sports facility and additional parking. These solutions were incorporated into the new general plan for redevelopment of the Village of Hempstead, which then provided a grounding for the Village of Hempstead Community Development Agency to request that the New York State Department of Transportation make needed improvements to the entrance to the village and adjoining existing streets.

ONE WAY
ONE WAY
ONE WAY

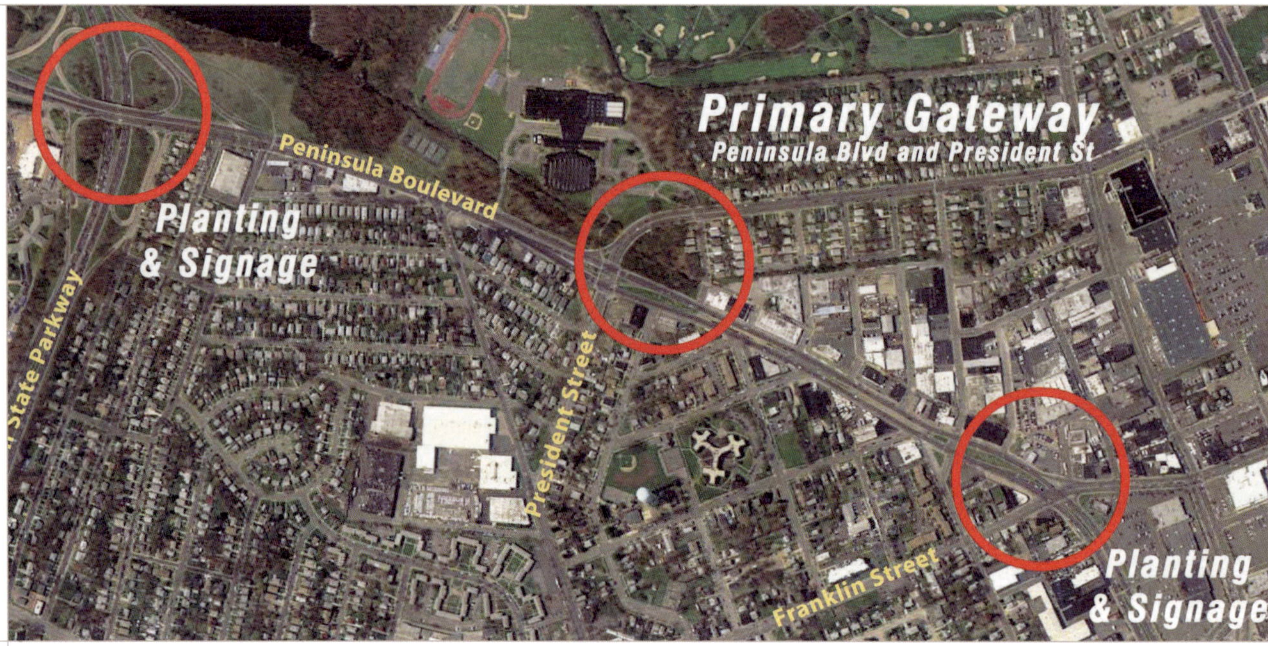

- STUDY AREA BEGINS AT THE SOUTHERN STATE PARKWAY
- RUNS NORTH ALONG PENINSULA BOULEVARD
- ENDING AT NORTH FRANKLIN AVENUE INTERSECTION

a

Aerial Photo, Proposed Roundabout

a. Concept Peninsula Boulevard.
b. Peninsula Boulevard, Cross Section.
c. Crossing and Gateway Town Center.

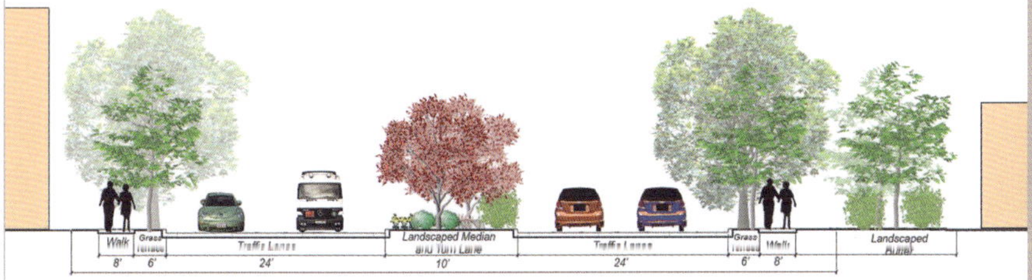

b

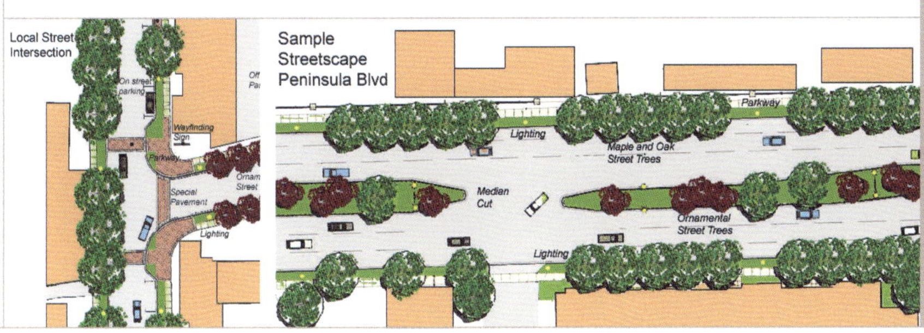

c

LA MARQUETA VISIONING PROJECT

CHAPTER 01

PARTNERS:

Harlem Community Development Corporation.
Chelsea Market.
Meta Brunzema Architects PC.
Community Board 11.

DATE OF PROJECT:

2002

The site of the La Marqueta Visioning Project includes the Park Avenue corridor, adjacent blocks facing the avenue, the Metro-North viaduct between 110th and 126th streets in East Harlem, and unbuilt space beneath the viaduct, including La Marqueta, a historic market situated beneath the viaduct between East 111th and 116th streets. The site was under the jurisdiction of New York State and New York City (through the Empire State Development Corporation and the New York City Department of Housing Preservation and Development) with New York State Department of Transportation easements for Metro-North. At the time of the project, the space contained parking for city agencies, hospitals and market buildings, most of which were vacant.

The development proposal expanded on the concept of La Marqueta to create a destination "mega-market" based on the area's links with food and immigrant cultures. The project would collect the best of every type of specialty food from ethnic neighborhoods throughout the city, providing small business ventures with space for production, sales, and distribution, thus creating a unique tapestry of the flavors, colors, and smells of multi-ethnic New York in a unique urban pedestrian market.

The plan included a business model for a nonprofit, self-sustaining umbrella entity to provide a small-business incubator, possibly structured as one or more commercial cooperatives subleasing to shopkeepers. The project could contain larger commercial or community-use nodes to respond to local needs.

The CCAC and partners created a master plan with three phases leading toward implementation. The Harlem Community Redevelopment Corporation is in the process of implementing the concept.

la Marqueta
MACK

Top. Existing conditions
Bottom. Section
Next page. Final presentation

SUMMARY

- The International Market Mile is a proposal to create a unique destination for Harlem, the City and the region that will revitalize the Upper Park Avenue Corridor.
- A mile of specialty food-related businesses will draw together the diverse cultures and communities that make up East Harlem and New York City.
- Harlem CDC proposes a comprehensive study to address land use, traffic, parking, and other relevant issues with the goal of developing a viable implementation plan for the International Market Mile.

LOCATION

- Park Avenue between East 110th and East 132nd Streets: property beneath the Metro-North viaduct and neighboring sites facing Park Avenue.
- Current uses beneath the viaduct include:
    - "La Marqueta" buildings, mostly vacant or demolished, between 111th-116th Streets
    - Parking and roadway between 116th-132nd Streets.
- Current uses of neighboring sites include:
    - Many vacant and parking lots below 125th Street
    - Some community gardens and recreation spaces
    - Loft/factory buildings above 125th Street
    - Mix of residential buildings - NYCHA and tenements below 116th Street, New Partnership Homes 116th-120th Streets
- The site under the viaduct is City-owned. Property is controlled by EDC ("La Marqueta"), DOT, and DCAS.

BUSINESS MODEL

- Bring together the best of every type of specialty and ethnic food business from Harlem and neighborhoods throughout the City.
- Create a mile of food production/wholesale/retail businesses -- drawing upon historic precedents of fresh food markets under viaducts in New York City.
- Provide individual, self-contained units or shops -- instead of stalls in open market halls.
- Manage units as a commercial coop -- businesses buy-in and share resources and costs, including delivery trucks and management IT System.
- Provide "ready-to-go" space for local new or expanded small-business ventures -- units of 1000-2000 s.f. for on site food production and retail.
- Create at least 900 local jobs: 750 production/retail jobs, 150 construction jobs.
- Spur additional economic development opportunities and job creation to allied industries in surrounding neighborhood.

BENEFITS TO NEIGHBORHOOD

- Re-energize the streetscape by opening businesses toward the street, creating a wider, covered circulation zone along Park Avenue under the viaduct and changing current "back-alley" of Park Avenue into a "front yard" between neighborhoods to the east and west.
- Create a focal point for the neighborhood, as well as adding to Harlem's growing international tourism, due to the market's strategic location.
- Activate space beneath the viaduct to spur development of facing sites for complementary commercial and production uses: ground-floor retail, restaurants, entertainment, and commercial office/production lofts above.
- Provide a catalyst for continued housing growth in surrounding neighborhoods, complementing existing and newly constructed residential units.

EAST RIVER GREENWAY

CHAPTER 01

PARTNERS:

Manhattan Community Board 3
Waterfront Task Force.
National Park Service Rivers and Trails Program.

DATE OF PROJECT:

2004

The enthusiasm and creativity that community members showed throughout the Community Design Workshop and planning process is an indicator that the waterfront is a high priority for Community District 3 residents. While a number of innovative concepts emerged from the workshop brainstorming sessions, the vast majority of these ideas – and certainly the principles and main themes – are compatible with the intent of city-wide planning for the waterfront over the past decade. CD3 residents crave the kind of public access and enjoyment of the waterfront that has been the intent of policy and design studies such as A Greenway Plan for New York City, the Plan for the Manhattan Waterfront (1993) and the East River Bikeway and Esplanade Master Plan Report (1996).

Results from the Community Design Workshop also align with the direction of the recently released report from the Rebuild Chinatown Initiative, entitled America's Chinatown: A Community Plan.

In the past few years, the City and other entities have made remarkable progress in taking waterfront plans from the schematic design phase to built spaces where New Yorkers enjoy biking, walking, sunbathing, kayaking and other activities. Although the waterfront on the Lower East Side has benefitted from this redevelopment, it still lags far behind many other sections of the Manhattan Greenway. The concept plan and principles for The East River Greenway express a vision that would reunite the diverse communities of the Lower East Side, Two Bridges and Chinatown neighborhoods with the estuarine environment that is now so geographically near and yet still remote due to physical barriers and design deficiencies.

The community's vision would not only create a vibrant edge on the Lower East Side, it would also have a positive impact on the environmental quality of these reaches of the East River Shoreline. The restoration of naturalized shoreline and new green space called for in the Concept Plan, along with pollution reduction and remediation

measures, would likely far outweigh any required mitigation for items such as new piers or the extension of existing piers.

The charrette prompted much far-sighted and positive visioning for the future. However, it is also important to note the kinds of uses the CD3 residents expressly avoided in their designs. Waterfront uses considered objectionable by community residents include:

- Uses, including commercial (retail or wholesale), which would generate an increase in truck and automobile traffic or noise.
- Uses that are not water-related and which would diminish access to the waterfront and block views.
- Housing.
- "Tourist Trap Destinations".

Other brainstorming ideas:

- Create wetland along the shoreline to remediate water pollution and run-off and to mitigate the impact of new piers.
- Modify DOS building at Pier 36 with green roof park on top (Example: Riverbank State Park).
- Add cascading planting on the FDR viaduct.

To return to the optimistic spirit of the Waterfront Design Workshop, an overall theme is the desire for authenticity and respect for the uniqueness of the Lower East Side and Chinatown as the destination for generations of immigrants from around the world. This sense of place should permeate every planning and design decision for the waterfront.

EAST RIVER GREENWAY
COMMUNITY DESIGN WORKSHOP

EAST RIVER GREENWAY CONCEPT PLAN

SUMMARY OF EAST RIVER GREENWAY COMMUNITY DESIGN WORKSHOP

LEGEND

- IMPROVED GREENWAY TRAIL
- CULTURAL / RECREATION DESTINATIONS
- ACTIVITY ZONE
- IMMEDIATE PUBLIC ACCESS
- EXTEND PIER FOR PUBLIC ACCESS
- WATERFRONT PROMENADE
- ACTIVITY AND AMENITY NODE
- BICYCLE ROUTES
- PRIMARY GREEN CORRIDOR
- SECONDARY GREEN CORRIDOR
- TERTIARY GREEN CORRIDOR
- "GREEN" EDGE
- PROPOSED BUS SERVICE
- 14 BUS LINE (PROPOSED EXTENSION)
- WATER TAXI
- SMALL BOATS
- INTERMODAL HUB
- 14A BUS LINE (EXISTING)
- 22 BUS LINE (EXISTING)
- 15 BUS LINE (EXISTING)
- EXISTING SUBWAY STATION

GREENING
THE GREENWAY

Principle:

"Green" this section of the East River Greenway and FDR corridor to reduce pollution and add "more nature".

Top. Proposed Plan
Bottom. Existing conditions

ALTERNATIVE
TRANSPORTATION

Principle:

Reduce noise, air and water pollution and hazards caused by vehicular traffic, while increasing clean, accessible forms of public transit,waterborne transportation and pedestrian and bicycle access to and along the waterfront.

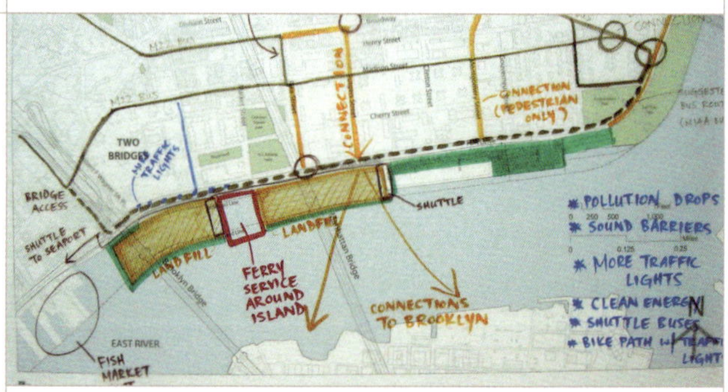

Top. Proposed Plan
Bottom. Existing conditions

VEHICULAR
ROUTES

Principle:

"Humanize" the FDR by making pedestrian safety and amenities a very high priority in all design and transportation decisions.

Top. Proposed Plan
Bottom. Existing conditions

WATERFRONT
DESTINATION

Principle:

The waterfront should be a primary cultural and recreational destination that will unite diverse neighborhood cultures.

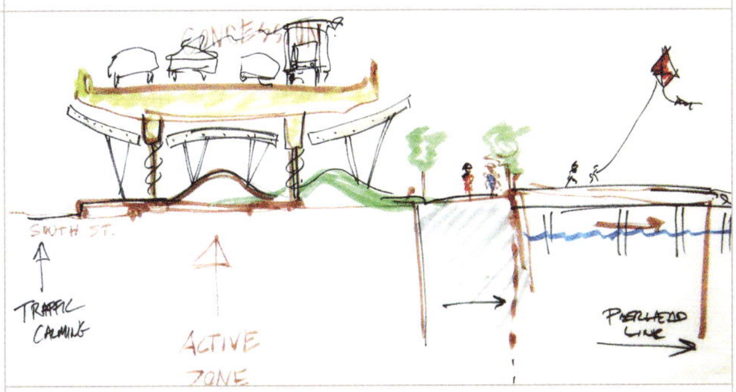

Top. Proposed Plan
Bottom. Existing conditions

BETWEEN BRIDGES

Principle:

Maximize space for public access along the water's edge for neighborhood residents.
Increase opportunities for visual and physical contact with the water.

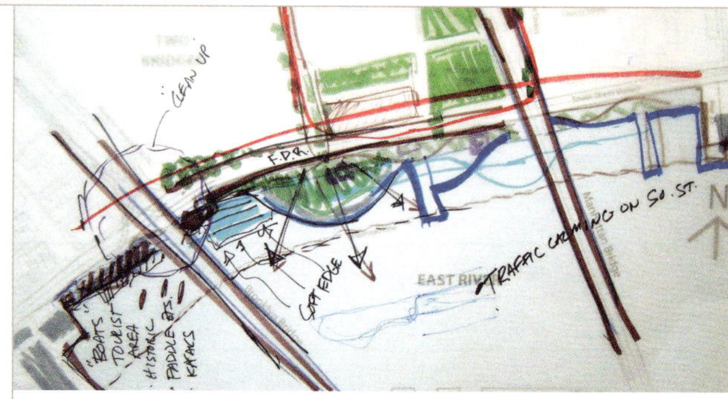

Top. Proposed Plan
Bottom. Existing conditions

THE PIERS

Principle:

Improve or redevelop piers to create opportunities for public access and recreation in keeping with the residential nature of the community. Any City or commercial facilities on the piers should contribute both in use and design to the health of local residents and the waterfront environment.

Brainstorming ideas for specific piers

PIER **35:**

- Open seasonal café on Pier 35.

PIER **36:**

- Modify DOS building with green roof and park on top (example: Riverbank State Park).
- Extend pier 36 out to pierhead line and add public access along edge.
- Redevelop pier 36 for velodrome.
- Keep DOS and EMS facilities in place for community services.
- Add permanent, year-round restaurant at Pier 36 or 42.

PIER **42:**

- Carve into edge near Pier 42; make it more park-like; add cultural venues, relating to East River Park and amphitheater.
- Create a Museum of the Lower East Side.
- Use part of pier 42 for environmental education exhibits about water and marine ecosystems.
- Renovate pier buildings for active use such as skate park or cycling.
- Add walkway connecting Pier 42 to East River Park along or over water (desire to "walk on water").
- Build a community compost facility along with educational component on a portion of the pier.

PIER **35/36,** existing condition.

PIER **36,** existing condition.

PIER **42,** existing condition.

PIER **44,** existing condition.

MONTEFIORE PARK & PLAZA

CHAPTER 01

PARTNERS:

Heritage Health and Housing.
Harlem Community Development Corporation.
Friends of Montefiore Park.
Community Board 9.

DATE OF PROJECT:

2008 - 2009

Along with Heritage Health and Housing and the Harlem Community Development Corporation, the CCAC helped produce a concept for this underutilized park area in response to a request for proposals from the New York City Department of Transportation Plaza Program. The CCAC developed a preliminary design to submit along with the application. Together, the sponsoring organizations secured letters of support from local community organizations and business owners near the park. The design proposed to eliminate Hamilton Place, a street that runs diagonally behind the park. Expanding the park over the bed of Hamilton Place addresses several safety and quality of life issues, including alleviating a pedestrian-vehicular conflict at the intersection of 138th Street and Hamilton Place (one of the gateways to City College) and exposing a homeless encampment adjacent to the PS 192 retaining wall.

Because the existing plan of the park discourages lingering, residents have creatively adapted by bringing their own plastic chairs and placing them in the pathways, impairing circulation. The proposed new design includes a terraced park that would provide informal seating on steps, level areas for entertainment, and a space for an open market or celebration of various events. The large trees would be preserved in their existing locations, and several small trees could be moved to create a more open space. The porous pavement suggested for the site filters stormwater runoff, thereby improving the environment and meeting several goals of the New York City mayor's PlaNYC initiative. The proposed improvements to Montefiore Park have gained the support of the Department of Transportation and the Department of Parks and Recreation, and the renovation work is scheduled to begin within the next four years.

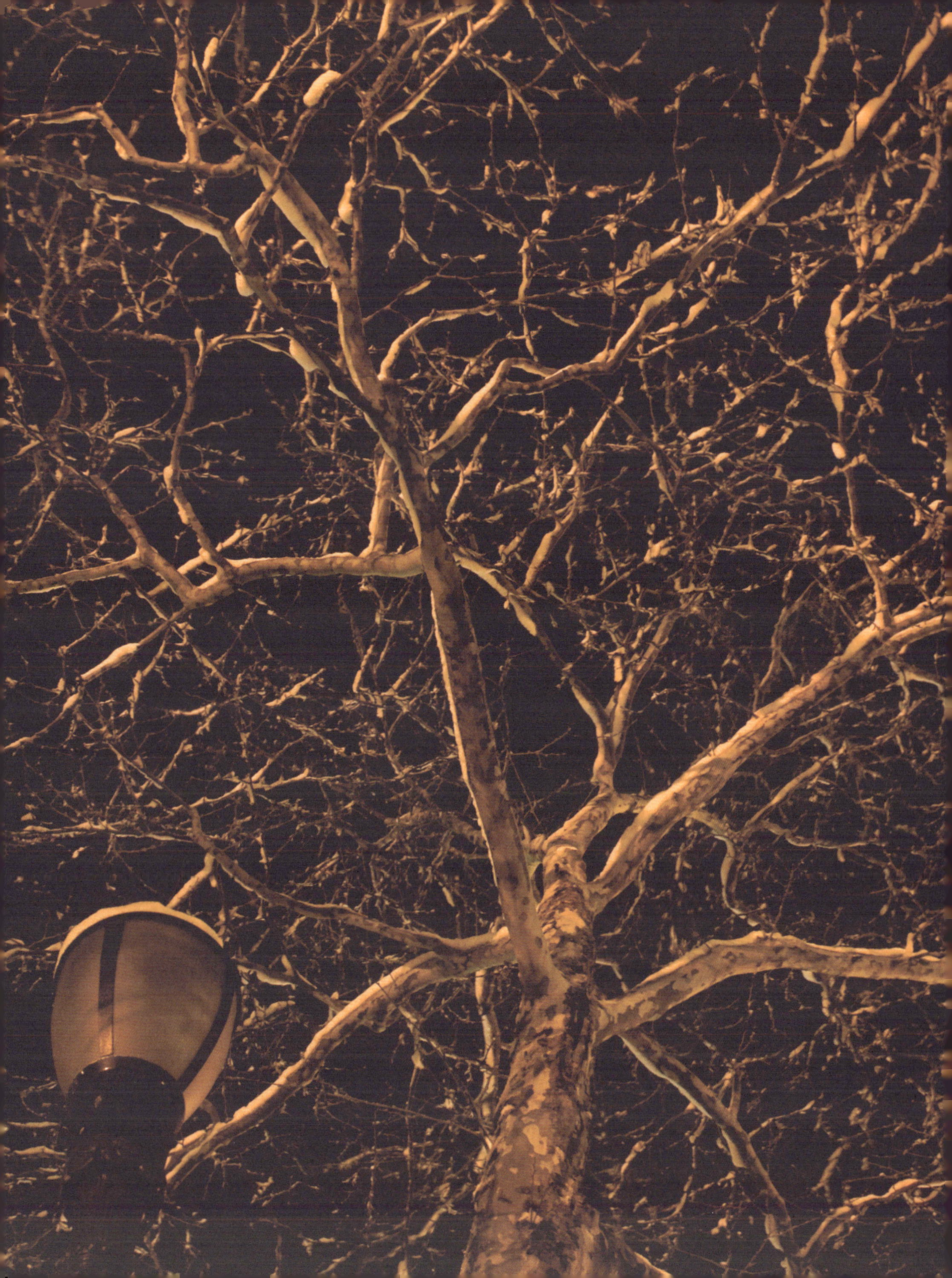

Top. Existing conditions
Next page. Proposed Plan
Below. Section

138TH STREET

PLANTED AREA SEATING STEPS PLAZA AMPHITHEATER MARKET PLACE

ROCKAWAY BEACH BRANCH GREENWAY

CHAPTER 01

PARTNERS:

Rockaway Beach Branch
Greenway Committee.

DATE OF PROJECT:

2008 - 2009

The Rockaway Beach Branch Greenway Committee asked the CCAC to map and document their Rails to Trails project, consisting of a portion of the disused Long Island Railroad line running from Rego Park to Ozone Park in Queens. The CCAC created a preliminary design for the greenway and prepared an informational brochure addressed to the community surrounding the trail to help start the funding campaign for the development phase of the project.

The Rockaway Beach Branch railway was built in 1880. It connected New York City residents to the Ocean Beaches of the Rockaway Peninsula, providing urban dwellers with access to the sea and its recreational opportunities. The right-of-way was abandoned by the Long Island Railroad in 1962. The train tracks and the adjacent land have become derelict open space. This vacant, forgotten land can be turned into a linear urban oasis.

PROPOSED ROCKAWAY BEACH BRANCH GREENWAY

a

ROCKAWAY BEACH BRANCH GREENWAY

The Rockaway Beach Branch Greenway Committee is determined to transform an abandoned right of way into a 3.5 mile long greenway corridor. Providing recreational, educational and transportation opportunities, it will also connect residential and commercial areas of Rego Park, Forest Hills, Richmond Hill, Ozone Park and Woodhaven."

b

Previous page. Proposed greenway
a. Sitting on a rock in the park
b. Pamphlet cover

CHAPTER 02

EXHIBIT

MANHATTANVILLE: HIDDEN IN PLAIN SIGHT

CHAPTER 02

PARTNERS:

Eric K. Washington.
Cohen Library, City College of New York.

DATE OF PROJECT:

2001 - 2002

The CCAC collaborated with Eric K. Washington, guest curator for this exhibit, which is based on Mr. Washington's 2002 book Manhattanville: Old Heart of West Harlem, along with his collections and research. The exhibit focuses on the Manhattanville neighborhood, its involvement in the Revolutionary War period, and its subsequent legacy as a residential, manufacturing, and transportation hub. The effect of the planning under the regime of Robert Moses is also examined, including the consequences of the destruction of a rich, multicultural fabric of residences to make way for homogenized housing projects.

12 Av

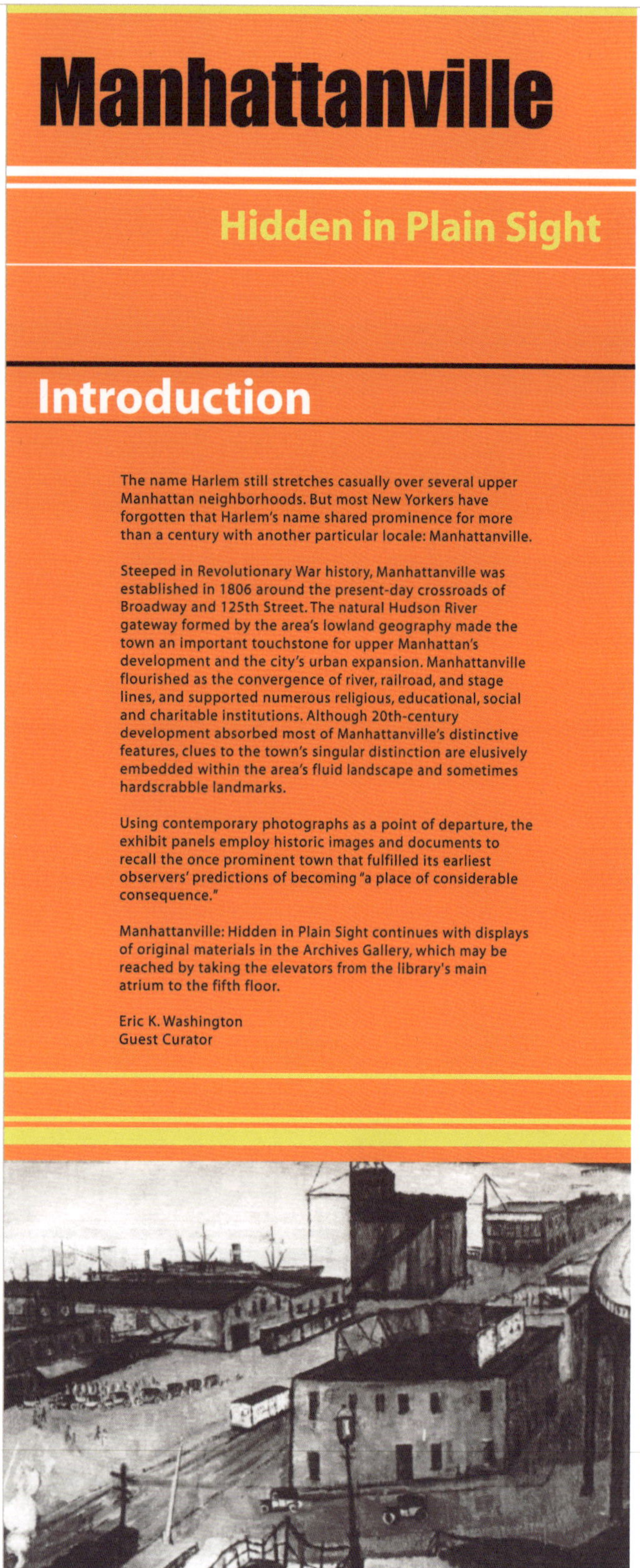

a

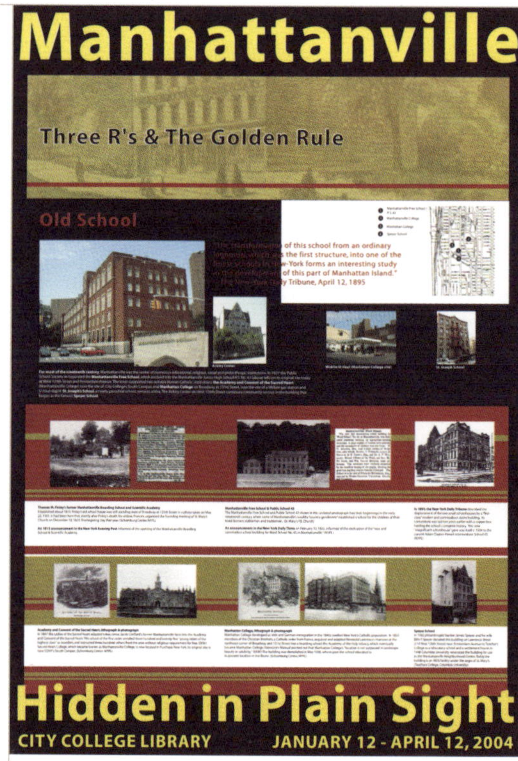

b

a. Introduction panel
b. Promotional postcard
c. Reception
d. Archives
e. Archives

c

d

e

CHANGING STREETSCAPES: NEW ARCHITECTURE & OPEN SPACE IN HARLEM

CHAPTER 02

PARTNERS:

Cohen Library, City College of New York.
NYC Department of Housing, Preservation and Development (HPD).

DATE OF PROJECT:

2005

This exhibit focused on some of the more prominent physical transformations in five areas of building and design in Harlem: residential, commercial, cultural and institutional, open space, and zoning.

It highlighted recent and projected transformations in Harlem neighborhoods and attempted to show the viewer those streetscapes that reflect new development dynamics:

- An ongoing, dramatic push on the part of the city to house all income levels within the community, starting with those most in need of subsidized housing and reaching out to those who only now are looking at Harlem as a viable residential alternative to other areas of Manhattan. Brand-new apartment buildings, town houses and substantially rehabilitated housing dot the streets and avenues, offering a new look in some cases and a spruced-up, though familiar look along some blocks.

- The expansion of retail and office space, answering the demand within a community with money to spend and offering employment to many, although perhaps to fewer than some would like. Commercial activity is attracting people from outside the community, and the look of the street is changing. Some are happier than others about this.

- The increased vitality of existing cultural and academic institutions that are stretching and growing and calling upon architects and planners to move them into the future. New museums are planning for their own presence in this vital community.

- New open spaces and parks, some being planned and others already welcoming the community onto their grounds. Streets and avenues are getting attention, and more and more sport new lampposts, historical plaques, statues, and greenery.

Top. ST. CHARLES CONDOMINIUMS.

HOUSING

MOUNT MORRIS PARK BRADHURST AREA BUILDING BLOCKS WEST 140TH, STREET WEST 148TH FREDERICK DOUGLASS BOULEVARD CORRIDOR LENOX AVENUE CORRIDOR MADISON AVENUE CORRIDOR

HOUSING

Housing abandonment and disinvestment swept across Harlem in the 1960s and 1970s, displacing residents and leaving thousands of housing units, countless vacant lots and entire blocks in city hands.
By the 1980s the New York City Department of Housing Preservation and Development (HPD) was the defacto owner of 60% of Harlem´s residential real estate due to tax delinquency and abandonment by owners.

c

a. Bradhurst Court, 300 - 316 West 145th Street
b. Mount Morris Park, 62 & 64 West 119th Street
c. Fifth Avenue Homes. Block bounded by East 118th, East 119th Streets and Madison and Fifth Avenues
d. Malcom Shabazz Gardens, west 117th Street
e. St. Charles Condominiums, Frederick Douglass Boulevard between West 136th and West 138th Streets
f. East side of Frederick Douglass boulevard between West 145th and West 146th Streets

d

e

a

b

f

Top. RIVERBANK STATE PARK

LANDSCAPE & OPEN SPACE

LAND & OPEN SPACE

Providing a setting for the building boom, civic groups, residents and elected officials have shown leadership and ingenuity in improving Harlem's open space network. These efforts extend from Harlem's historic landscape parks revealing Upper Manhattan's rugged terrain, to the infrastructure of its streets and boulevards, and its abundant shoreline. Neighborhood coalitions and "Friends" groups have been instrumental in adopting parks to assist with safety, clean-up and seeking outside funds to supplement over-stretched Parks Department budgets. The Historic Harlem Parks initiative is one of four "catalyst programs" of Partnerships for Parks, a public/private venture that provides capacity building support and community organizing around programming and targeted improvements in Jackie Robinson Park, Marcus Garvey Park, St. Nicholas Park and Morningside Park (pictured above, clockwise from top). "Take Me to the River," an initiative sponsored by Borough President C. Virginia Fields, the Riverside Park Fund, the West Harlem Art Fund and a coalition of community groups has engaged in planning to improve access to the Hudson River in Riverside Park north of 145th Street.

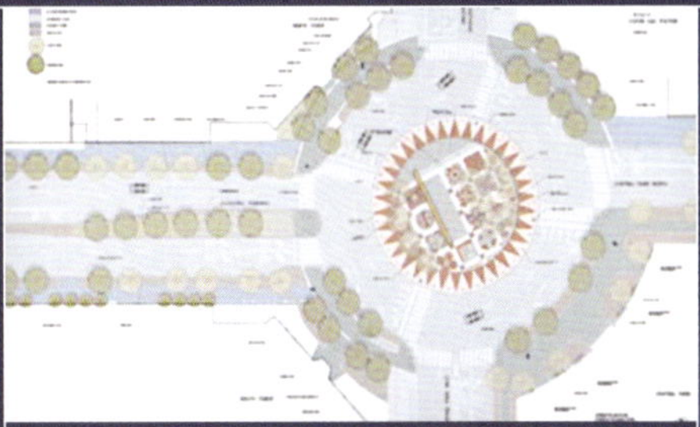
b

c

d

e

a

a. Ralph Ellison Memorial
b. Harlem Gateway / Frederick Douglass Circle
c. Malcolm X Plaza and Malcom X Boulevard Improvements
d. Harlem River Park
e. West Harlem Piers Masterplan and Waterfront Park
f. Riverbank State Park

f

INSTITUTIONS
CULTURE, EDUCATION AND SERVICE

Top. HARLEM HEALTH CENTER

INSTITUTIONS
CULTURE, EDUCATION AND SERVICE

Accompanying the development in residential and commercial areas are noticeable changes in the institutional landscape.
The first newly constructed public high school in Harlem in 50 years opened its doors in February 2004. The Thurgood Marshall Academy now stands where Small's Paradise once welcomed jazz lovers at West 135th Street and Adam Clayton Powell, Jr. Boulevard.
Nonprofit groups are responsible for some of the most striking new architecture. Harlem Children's Zone is a comprehensive social service organization that has built its new headquarters, which will include a charter school, at Madison Avenue and East 125th Street. The 10-story building offering a glassy facade to Hancock Place at 125th Street and Morningside Avenue is devoted to health care for hotel and restaurant workers, provided by their unions.

b

c

d

a

a. Former Cohen Library
b. Studio Museum in Harlem
c. Harlem Children's Zone
d. New York Structural Biology Center

Top. HARLEM USA

COMMERCIAL DEVELOPMENT

COMMERCIAL DEVELOPMENT

The upsurge in commercial activity is most evident on 125th Street. "Superstores" are anchoring new developments, as national retailers are eager to tap under-served, urban markets like Harlem. Local entrepreneurs, national chains and franchises are also changing the look of Harlem's avenues and major cross streets like 116th, 135th and 145th Streets. However, change is not always welcome as some residents raise concerns about the continuing viability of smaller, long-time merchants.

a

a. Harlem Park
b. Pathmark
c. Harlem Auto Mall
d. Uptown NY
e. Gotham Plaza

b

c

d

e

AMSTERDAM AVENUE
MAIN STREET REVITALIZATION

CHAPTER 02

PARTNERS:

Heritage Health and Housing.
West Harlem Group Assistance.
New York Main Street Program.

DATE OF PROJECT:

2008 - 2009

Upper Manhattan is in the midst of a rapid transformation. From Columbia University north through Harlem and into Washington Heights, investment has spurred economic revival in some of the most blighted parts of the city. This renewed interest has been concentrated, however, yielding pockets of revitalization amid the larger neglected neighborhood fabric.

A grant made through the New York Main Street Program offered an opportunity to encourage investment in parts of the upper Manhattan that have not yet seen much recovery. Equally important, the Main Street grant has helped Heritage Health and Housing (HHH) and its primary community partner West Harlem Group Assistance (WHGA) steer the resurgence in a direction that accommodates those who currently live and work in the community. Recognizing that some of the recent development in the area had already displaced residents and business owners, HHH/WHGA are using their influence to advocate a measured approach to gentrification.

The Main Street project focuses on the Amsterdam Avenue corridor, one of the most visible areas of Harlem that has yet to recover from decades of "benign" neglect. The corridor stretches from 140th Street to 145th Street and includes the Johnny Hartman Plaza at the intersection of Hamilton Place and Amsterdam.

The six-block grant area is a neighborhood of mixed-use buildings of harmonious, consistent design, based on nearly identical building modules that are enlivened by

D
S
1753
HOT & COLD
SADWICHES
OLD BEERS
STOP
FREE DELIVERY
PHARMACY
ONE

an exceptional portfolio of elegant nineteenth-century architectural treatments. Many of the corridor's blocks are occupied by pairs of long five-story buildings, which typically have four stories of residential units over ground-floor commercial units. There are twenty-six residential buildings and fifty-one commercial units in the corridor, with between six and thirteen storefronts per block. The corridor is also punctuated and enhanced by several potentially attractive public green spaces. There are no empty lots within this area; at the time of the project, there were fourteen vacant storefronts, three of which had new or anticipated leases.

The goals of the Amsterdam Avenue Main Street project were to display ideas for organizing and structuring the streetscape in a way that would be visually legible, inviting, and user friendly; to promote economic revitalization and development within the corridor; to identify, prioritize, and resolve problems recognized by the community; to provide an opportunity for community artists to contribute to the enhancement of the streetscape; to support the preservation and general enhancement of the existing retail spaces and housing stock; and to promote Harlem's past, present, and future in a positive way by embracing the history and culture of its residents.

The following sites were selected as demonstration projects, and plans for their renovation were shown in the exhibition:

1681-7 Amsterdam Avenue (447 West 143rd Street)

This building is typical of the architectural design along the Amsterdam corridor, with about ninety feet on the ground level dedicated to four storefronts and four stories of apartments above. Its corner location places its two visible sides in the Hamilton Heights Historic District. The Amsterdam Avenue corridor project proposed replacing the current awnings over the R&R Neighborhood Grocery storefront on the corner of the building with new ones that comply with historic district criteria. It would also replace the grocery's closed-panel security gates with open-link gates and install energy-saving LED outdoor lighting. The store's interior would be enhanced and reorganized for the customers' convenience. Similar landmark-criteria awnings and open-link gates were proposed for the three stores that adjoin the grocery.

At the building's Amsterdam and West 143rd Street facade, multicolored paints that covered the walls at the ground level would be removed, exposing the original limestone. Brickwork and masonry would be repaired as needed on the entire facade; in addition, the residential entry door on 143rd Street visible from Amsterdam Avenue would be replaced, and security lighting would be installed along the facades.

132-142 HAMILTON PLACE

(FACING JOHNNY HARTMAN PLAZA AT AMSTERDAM AVENUE)

Of the building's four storefronts, two were vacant at the time the project began. The CCAC proposed interior work as needed in the vacant 600-square-foot storefronts. Awning and gate upgrades were proposed for the facade, similar to that for the R&R Grocery, along with interior renovation.

501 WEST 143RD STREET

The building's entrance doors would be replaced and security lighting along the facade would be installed. West Harlem Group Assistance, which owns the building and the Hope Stevens Garden on 142nd Street and Amsterdam Avenue, plans to make facade improvements on four storefronts and upgrade the garden with planting and brickwork.

MISHKIN'S DRUGSTORE

The 100-plus-year-old landmark store at Amsterdam Avenue and 145th Street was targeted for facade and interior enhancement.

JAVA'S BREWIN'

Located at the corner of 140th Street and Amsterdam Avenue, the coffee shop would use project grant money to install an inviting a sidewalk café.

Top. Amsterdam Avenue &143rd Street N. E. corner
Bottom. 1658-1660 Amsterdam Avenue

Existing condition

Proposed

Existing condition

Proposed

AMSTERDAM AVENUE
MODEL

AMSTERDAM AVENUE
EXHIBIT

CHAPTER 03

PLANNING STUDIES

NORTHERN MANHATTAN
HERITAGE PLAN

CHAPTER 03

PARTNERS:

Project Funded by a grant from the National Endowment for the Arts.

DATE OF PROJECT:

2002 - 2004

The CCAC conducted a study of strategic planning and urban design opportunities around heritage-based themes in Northern Manhattan, primarily in the neighborhoods of Manhattanville, West Harlem / Hamilton Heights, Washington Heights, and Inwood, with the goal of finding ways to engage the Northern Manhattan community's history and heritage as a basis for strategizing about its future.

The intention of the study was to:

- Foster discussion around a range of challenging issues that inevitably emerge from a community defining its history and contemporary identity.
- Produce a final report for broad public distribution that would document research and findings and suggestions for coherent themes and area boundaries.
- Recommend next steps for design, preservation, and educational programs and for identifying and attracting needed resources.

Some particular objectives of the study and overall heritage plan included:

- Identifying historical and cultural themes and subjects that link places, events, activities, and people as part of the visible and past fabric of Northern Manhattan's varied communities.
- Identifying public places where design, quality, and amenities can be enhanced and improved.
- Suggesting strategies to improve selected public places and areas in order to strengthen the present-day experience of place and heritage.

- Identifying opportunities and resources for funding recommended improvements and enhancements.
- Highlighting existing educational programs and identifying areas for new activities that will strengthen the knowledge and understanding of Northern Manhattan among residents and visitors.
- Highlighting existing examples of interpretive programming or projects within the community and among local groups and institutions, as well as recommending additional opportunities to increase public awareness.

In conducting the study, the CCAC first created an inventory of cultural resources and historical sites in the area and analyzed the physical and social makeup of these communities. The CCAC then defined historical themes and areas of interest, developed a walking tour of the area, complete with map, provided urban design proposals and GIS maps, and produced a report of its findings. Specific activities during the initial study and subsequent development of the heritage plan included:

- Compiling available histories of Northern Manhattan and documenting its physical development and growth over time.
- Inventorying existing physical conditions, including land use, architecture and infrastructure, streetscape conditions, open space, physical connections or barriers, and transportation.
- Conducting and recording field observations within neighborhoods, along commercial corridors, and in the areas surrounding historical and cultural destinations.
- Reviewing available demographic and census data.
- Researching models, precedents, and best practices used in other communities' heritage or cultural district planning.
- Inventorying community, historical, and cultural institutions, organizations, resources, and activities.
- Convening and engaging community stakeholders in a variety of venues to obtain their participation and input.
- Documenting actual and perceived boundaries and identities of neighborhoods within the area.
- Developing unifying themes based on data collection, research, and observation.

Assembling this information in a single report allowed for a synthesis of many issues that had not been presented simultaneously in this way before.

The Northern Manhattan study generated important follow-up projects with which the CCAC also became involved, including producing a land use study for Washington Heights and Inwood; working on proposals to designate landmark districts, such as Audubon Terrace; authoring the Sherman Creek: Visions/Visiones study; and creating tourist maps for the central Harlem and Sugar Hill areas.

NEW YORK
HERITAGE PROGRAM

THE NEW YORK STATE HERITAGE AREAS SYSTEM BACKGROUND AND OVERVIEW

The New York State Heritage Area System dates back two decades to a program first established in 1982 under the rubric of the "Urban Cultural Park System." In 1994, the program was officially renamed the New York State Heritage Areas System. Throughout the two decades of its existence, the Heritage Areas System has been administered by the New York State Office of Parks, Recreation, and Historic Preservation (OPRHP).

THE INTENTIONS OF THE PROGRAM ARE SPELLED OUT BY OPRHP UNDER FOUR GOALS:

- Preservation of natural and historic resources.
- Recreational use of these resources.
- Education about local and regional heritage.
- Economic revitalization through public and private reinvestment.

(Source: OPRHP "New York State Heritage Area" fact sheet)

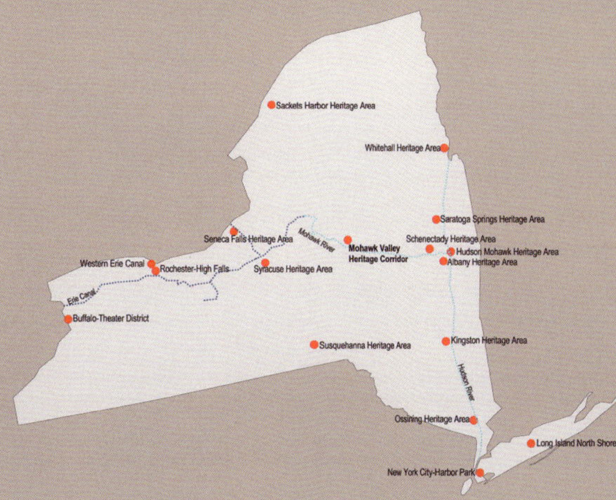

NATIONAL HERITAGE AREA MAP

NY RIVERS

MOHAWK RIVER
THE ERIE CANAL
THE HUDSON RIVER
NEW YORK STATE HERITAGE
NEW YORK

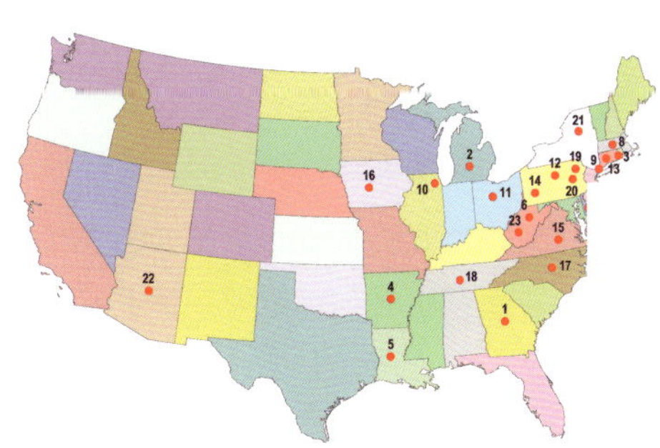

NEW YORK STATE HERITAGE AREA SYSTEM

HISTORICAL TIMELINE OF NORTHERN MANHATTAN

The historical timeline presented over the next few pages illustrates episodes in the rich history of Northern Manhattan, tracing some of the events that contributed to the story of the development and activities of the communities of Northern Manhattan. The timeline represents only a sampling from the 400 year written history of this area. In order to organize these events and to suggest opportunities for potential coordination among historically based initiatives, we clustered events into categories or periods organized by theme, as indicated in the summary timeline on the right. In the pages that follow, we elaborate on each period with specific events that fall under the various headings.

Pre. 1600

Indian settlements flourished for thousands of years before European visitors and settlers arrived in the Northern Manhattan. There were many Lenape and other Indian habitation sites and trails, fragments of which are in existence in Inwood Hill Park. The trails were later used by Europeans, and were incorporated into roadways such as Broadway and St. Nicholas Avenue.

European Settlers:
1649 - 1818

Although roads, transportation, and settlements were scarce, a few families, most of them wealthy, established their estates in Upper Manhattan, becoming the area's first European inhabitants. The end of this period is marked by surveys, e.g. the 1811 Commisioners Map, to lay out streets, roads, and public squares throughout most of Manhattan.

Shifts in Ownership
c.1600 - 1683

After Europeans first explored the New York region, ownership and political control of Northern Manhattan fluctuated with great frequency for almost a century. The land passed from the native peoples to the Dutch and then to the English, and in and out of the borders of New York City as its boundaries changed.

Revolutionary War
1776 - 1783

Northern Manhattan passed out of civilian and into military control during the American Revolution. Most residents had already abandoned their homes when Washington's army retreated through the area. British forces assumed military control over the practically deserted territory, constructing several forts throughout the area. Civilian control returned with the British evacuation in 1783.

Rural Refuge in a Growing City

1818 - 1865

As downtown Manhattan grew more and more crowded, some New Yorkers utilized the still open spaces of Upper Manhattan for summer homes. This rural refuge also began to be occupied by industries, institutions and other establishments requiring large areas of land and isolation from the densely populated city.

Migration and Immigration

1880 - Present

At the end of the 19th century, European immigrants from Germany, Ireland, Italy, Russia and elsewhere moved uptown to find relief from the crowded downtown tenements. In the first decades of the 20th century, the great migration of African-Americans from the South and the Caribbean to Harlem and Northern Manhattan created the largest community of blacks in New York and in any city in the U.S. Thousands of new Jewish immigrants arrived in the 1930s-40s, fleeing from Europe in the years before World War II. Throughout the 20th century, waves of Hispanic groups—first Puerto Ricans, later Cubans, Dominicans and others – found homes and created new communities.

Urbanization - The City Expands

1875 - 1931

Largely due to the construction of elevated railways in the 1870s and the subway lines in the first decade of the 20th century, Northern Manhattan developed at a faster rate than at any other point in its history. By 1930, the area had become completely urban.

Reconstruction and Resilience

1931 - Present

The construction of multi-family dwellings, both large private apartment buildings and public housing projects, continued in Northern Manhattan through the 1970s, and to some extent to the end of the 20th century. Massive public works projects, especially transportation structures, transformed the scale of the built environment.

PHYSICAL
DEVELOPMENT

Built Structures
(Farms, Forts, Buildings)

These "figure-ground" diagrams represent the evolution of the built fabric of Northern Manhattan. The 1782 map shows the location of villages, farms and fortifications at the time of the Revolutionary War. Buildings are scattered along the main road, which is roughly the route of Broadway today. More settlement is evident in 1851, although the area is still mostly rural. The villages of Manhattanville at the western end of 125th Street and Harlem to the east appear as clusters of development, as do settlements around Coogan's Bluff (155th Street). Institutions begin to locate in the area during the latter half of the 19th century – the New York Juvenile Asylum in 1851 and the Washington Heights Private Library in 1868. Hamilton Heights, between Amsterdam and St. Nicholas Avenues from 140th to 150th Street, was developed between 1886 and 1906, as were the flat parcels along Broadway. The 1974 map indicates the dense neighborhoods and major open spaces we see today.

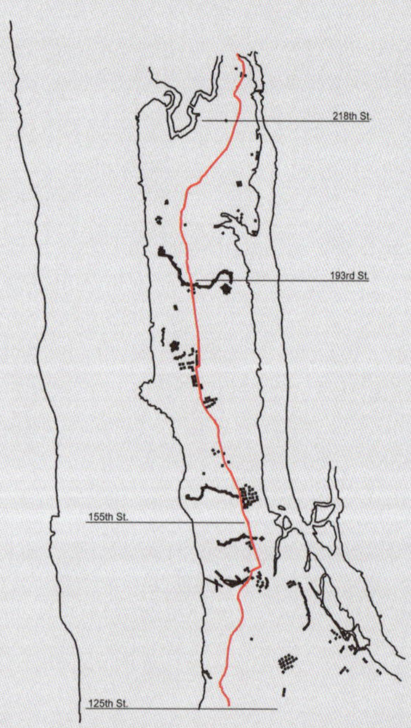

1782

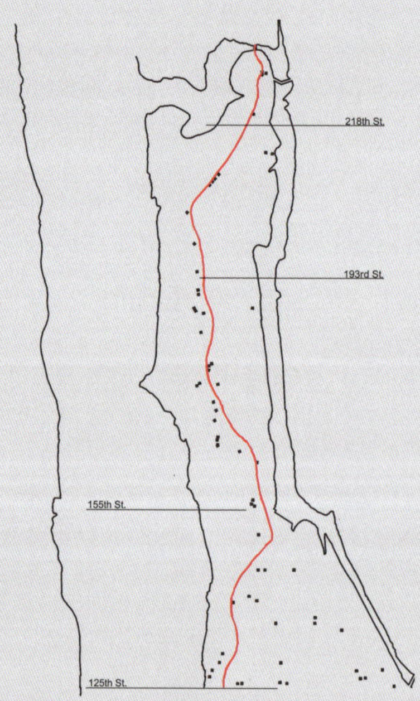

1807

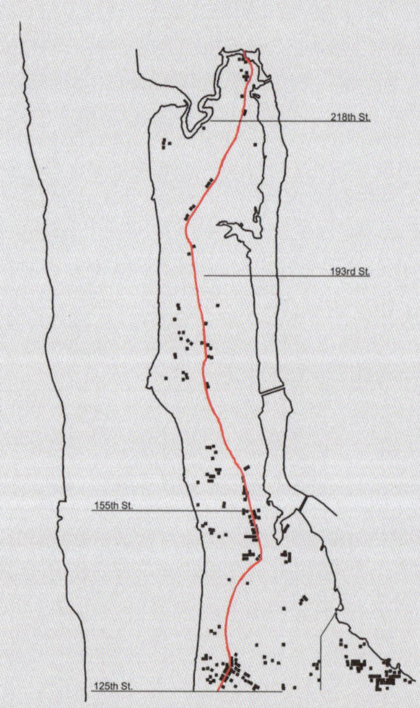

1851

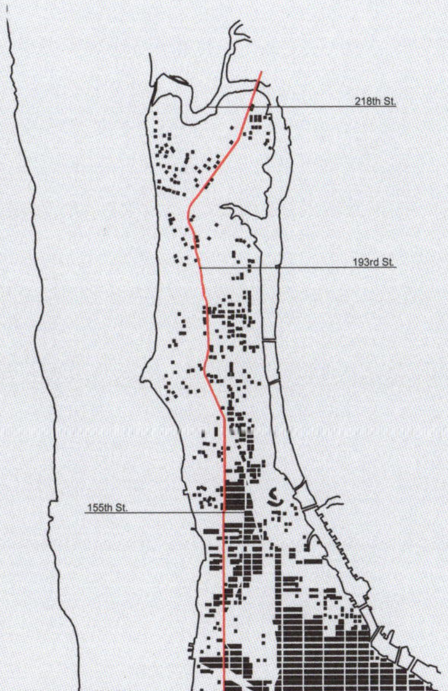

218th St.
193rd St.
155th St.
125th St.

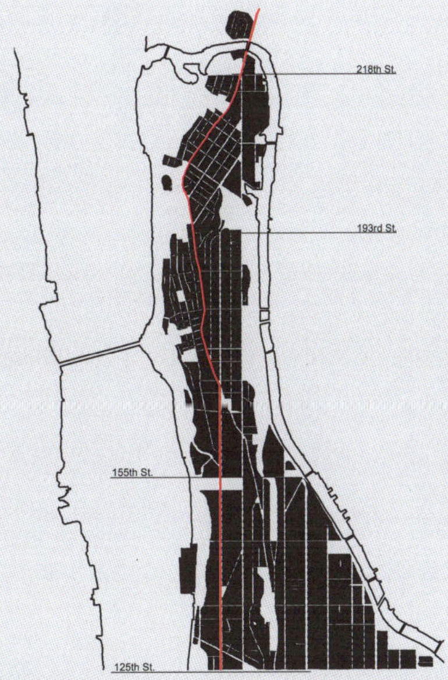

218th St.
193rd St.
155th St.
125th St.

1900

1974

1931 - PRESENT
RECONSTRUCTION AND RESILIENCE

During this period, the construction of multi-family dwellings, both large private apartment buildings and public housing projects, continued in Northern Manhattan through the 1970s, and to some extent to the end of the 20th century. Massive public works projects, especially transportation structures, transformed the scale of the built environment.

a. Brochure for Castle Village Apartments, 1939. www.seroy.com
b. North River Water Pollution Control Plant, c.1980s. www.nyc.gov
c. Building of the George Washington Bridge, c.1927. www.panynj.org
d. Inwood Hill Park
e. Inwood

a

1930s
The Hebrew Tabernacle of Washington Heights is constructed at 185th Street and Fort Washington Avenue.

1935
John D. Rockefeller donates Fort Tryon Park, designed by Frederick Law Olmsted, Jr., to the City.

1936
Harlem River Houses, from 151st to 153rd Streets, Macombs Place to the Harlem River, the first federal public housing project in New York City, is built for poor Harlem residents.

1938
The Metropolitan Museum of Art constructs the Cloisters in Fort Tryon Park. The building was reassembled from parts of several different medieval Spanish and French cloisters.

1930 **1945** **1960**

1931
The George Washington Bridge, designed by Chief Engineer O.H. Ammann and Architect Cass Gilbert, is completed at 178th Street and Fort Washington Avenue, connecting Northern Manhattan and Fort Lee, New Jersey.

1932
The IND Eighth Avenue subway line is completed in Washington Heights, running from Midtown to 207th Street. The new subway line spurs development west of Broadway, largely in the form of Art Deco apartments.

1939
Charles V. Paterno builds Castle Village on Cabrini Boulevard north of 181st Street facing Hudson View Gardens, an early coop apartment complex built by the Paterno family along the west side of Pinehurst Avenue between 183rd and 185th Streets.

Late 1930s - early 1940s
Developers build Art Deco style apartments in Washington Heights and Inwood to appeal to the current tastes of the middle class.

b

c

d

e

1941
Inwood Hill Park comes into its present configuration as the last of the City's land acquisitions are completed.

1945
Art Deco buildings in Washington Heights are now considered "showy, frivolous, and expensive." Developers begin building apartments in the International Style.

1963
The George Washington Bridge Bus Station opens between Fort Washington and Wadsworth Avenues, 178th Street and 179th Streets, linking the George Washington Bridge with the IND Eighth Avenue subway.

1976
Riverside Park Community Apartments are built at 3333 Broadway, between 133rd and 135th Streets.

1991
The rebuilding of the North River Water Pollution Control Plant is completed from 137th to 145th Streets, with the rooftop Riverbank State Park added in response to community concerns.

1975 **1990**

1960s
In the late 1960s, the Mendel Gottesman Library (1967) and the Science Center of the Belter Graduate School of Science (1968) are added to the Yeshiva University campus along Amsterdam Avenue between 183rd and 187th Streets. The main building at Amsterdam Avenue and 187th Street was constructed in 1928; domes, towers, and turrets can be seen from miles away.

1964
Residential towers, the Bridge Apartments, are built between Wadsworth and Audubon Avenues from 178th to 179th Streets over I-95, an early experiment in residential air rights over a highway.

1940s-1990s
Over five decades, new buildings and pavilions are added to the Columbia-Presbyterian Medical Center. Buildings that were erected during this time include the Julius and Armand Hammer Health Sciences Center (1979) at Fort Washington Avenue and 168th Street, the Lawrence G. Kolb Research Building (1987) at 168th Street and Haven Avenue, and the Psychiatric Institute/New York State Office of Mental Health (1998) at Riverside Drive and 165th Street.

1996
The former Mary Woodard Lasker Biomedical Research Building, originally the Audubon Theater and Ballroom, where Malcolm X was assassinated in 1965, is altered and a new building is added. The building, located at Broadway and West 165th Street, still presents its terracotta-glazed polychrome facade along Broadway.

WASHINGTON HEIGHTS & INWOOD PLANNING STUDY

CHAPTER 03

PARTNERS:

Community Board 12.
Harlem Community Development Corporation.
Office of the Manhattan Borough President Scott Stringer.
New York State Senator Eric Schneiderman.
New York City Councilman Robert Jackson.
Citibank.

DATE OF PROJECT:

2004 - 2008

Lower-income groups in New York City are finding the road to economic advancement blocked. The consequence of growing inequality is falling adversely on these residents, especially in the housing sector.

The elected officers of Community District 12, which includes Washington Heights and Inwood, were anxious to improve the economic health of their community and encourage appropriate development. They felt that the neighborhood provided important opportunities for development, based on three essential characteristics:

- Washington Heights/Inwood is a major population center with an extraordinary stock of residential architecture, constructed for the most part prior to 1947.
- The area has open-space resources that together are equivalent in area to Central Park: the three major parks (Highbridge, Inwood Hill, and Fort Tryon), which look outward to river views, have given the area the nickname "Upstate Manhattan".
- The area contains three major commercial and institutional hubs serving the community and the region: the Inwood central business district (CBD), the George Washington Bridge CBD (linking the north and south portions of St. Nicholas Avenue), and the Health Hub CBD, with its convenience "bowtie" commercial centers around the New York–Presbyterian Hospital campus.

Beginning in October 2005, Washington Heights and Inwood planning and community development organizations, in consultation with the CCAC, conducted research and field studies to identify and define a broad range of issues that affect Community District 12's physical, social, and economic development. They sought to create

a process to help them identify priority issues and develop a consensus opinion on community development, which could then provide the basis for the community board's support or opposition to proposed actions.

The process included:

- Initial conversations regarding goals and objectives, review of previous studies, and a field study examining current land uses and building conditions. In addition, a public opinion survey was conducted to identify major issues, the location of physical problems, and the community leaders and residents who have personal knowledge of and experience with these issues. Finally, a series of briefing reports was prepared for the district's standing committees, informing them of the study and survey findings and seeking consensus on the study's goals and objectives.
- Several presentations were held to exhibit the initial information gathered and show the CCAC's preliminary analysis of the social characteristics and vital statistics of Community District 12. These presentations provided a detailed review of land use and zoning, including the identification of three case study sites. Possible development scenarios for residential structures in each case study site were created using current and alternative zoning envelopes.
- Workshops were conducted for residents, political representatives, and community leaders. Four areas of interest were explored, including (1) preservation of affordable housing, (2) community parks and waterfront access, (3) district character and historic resources, and (4) community economic development. In addition, an open forum was held to allow identification of other issues and concerns. A final workshop featured the CCAC's preliminary recommendations for action. These workshops were designed by the CCAC to aid in demystifying the development resources offered through the inclusionary zone option and to examine the architectural impact of a range of options that might be chosen by developers.

Using the study findings, the CCAC helped the New York City Department of Housing Preservation and Development and Department of City Planning to develop a strategic plan and development policy for the area.

As part of the study, the CCAC also produced a set of goals and recommendations drawn from the synthesis of demographic research, field observation, a review of previous studies, and extensive public engagement conducted through interviews, questionnaires, and interactive workshops. From among the many recommendations put forward, the study selected thirty-one specific actions that it believed would best support the community's goals. Community Board 12 was encouraged to look carefully at these recommendations and select for implementation those actions that would help move the entire process of development and preservation forward. Setting priorities and promoting a mixed strategy of quick actions (picking the "low hanging fruit") and longer term, more substantial changes will help the community achieve the goals set by the studies. The CCAC evaluated several of these recommendations for the cost of implementation and provided cost estimates for each, together with a total cost for the entire package of recommendations.

To summarize study findings and recommendations, the CCAC prepared The Washington Heights and Inwood Planning and Land Use Study Report, published in March 2008. The first part of the report provided an overview of existing conditions and trends, while the second examined options available to Community Board 12 in its work to help build a resilient and diverse community. These options formed the framework of an overarching plan for decision making and action taking. This strategy allowed for a continuing review of conditions, intended to keep the plan alive and sufficiently flexible to meet new situations as they arise. Using these tools, community board policy statements could be used to help identify individual projects as either hindering or contributing to the solution of community development problems.

STUDY GOALS

The study goals emerged from the goals and objectives CB12 laid out in its original request-for-proposals in articulating its rationale for commissioning a district-wide planning study. Over the course of the study and in consultation with the Land Use Committee, the Project Team refined the language of these goals while seeking to address the original spirit of the RFP. The study seeks to address six goals, which informed the research and provided an organizing structure for this document:

1.

IDENTIFY TRENDS IN THE COMMUNITY AND BEST PRACTICES FOR BALANCED COMMUNITY DEVELOPMENT

- Provide information on who lives in CB12 and what their needs are.
- Develop a framework of priorities and potential actions towards assisting CB12 in fulfilling its mission.

2.

FOSTER DEVELOPMENT AND PRESERVATION OF AFFORDABLE HOUSING

- Encourage a mix of rental and ownership housing.
- Preserve the existing affordable housing inventory.

3.

LOCATE SITES/AREAS, AND ACTIONS, MEETING COMMUNITY NEEDS

- Include locations for housing, education and other community facilities; expansion of small business and economic activity; culture and recreation.

4.

PRESERVE AND STRENGTHEN DISTRICT CHARACTER AND QUALITY OF LIFE

- Highlight community assets and resources.
- Safeguard against over-development.

5.

LOCATE BUILDINGS AND AREAS OF SPECIAL ARCHITECTURAL OR HISTORIC INTEREST

- Identify buildings and districts for protection through landmark designation.
- Recommend alternative forms of protection or recognition.

6.

UPDATE ZONING

- Implement contextual zoning where appropriate.
- Reconcile existing zoning with actual land use and building form, while encouraging desired development patterns.

GOALS
1, 2 & 3

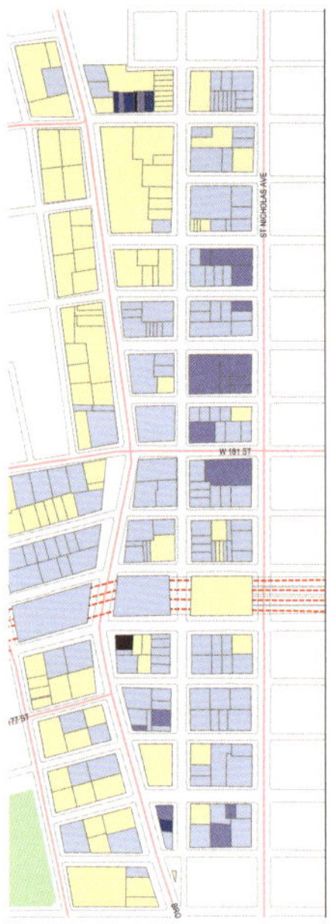

BUILDING CONDITIONS

- EXCELLENT
- GOOD
- FAIR
- POOR
- CRITICAL

OCCUPANCY

- OCCUPIED
- VACANT
- SEE OTHER NOTES
- 2ND FLOOR COMMERCIAL

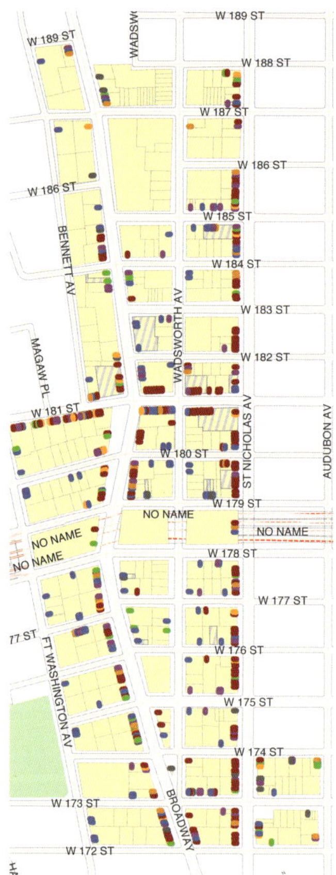

BUILDING CONDITIONS

- BANK
- CLOTHING AND SHOES
- JEWELRY AND ACCESSORIES
- SHOPPING
- ENTERTAINMENT
- RESTAURANTS
- FOOD
- GROCERY
- HAIR SALON
- PERSONAL SERVICES
- MEDICAL OFFICES
- OFFICES
- TRAVEL AGENCY
- OTHER
- COMMERCIAL 2 FLOOR

COMMERCIAL AND INSTITUTIONAL HUBS

WASHINGTON HEIGHTS SURVEY

SURVEY AREA BUILDING CONDITIONS AND OCCUPANCY

COMMERCIAL AND INSTITUTIONAL HUBS

INVENTORY OF COMMERCIAL SPACES

SURVEY AREA BUSINESS TYPES

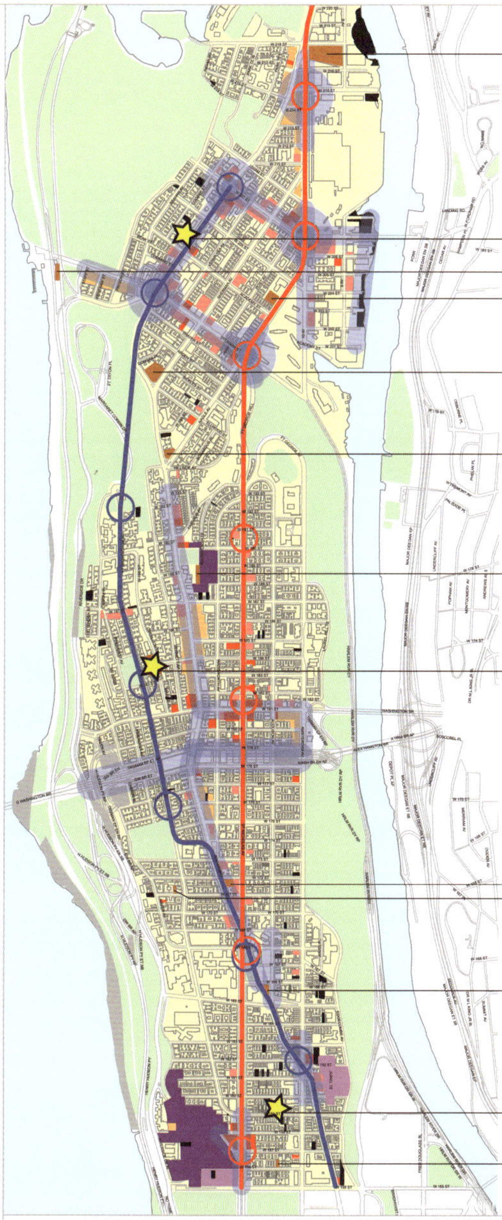

DEVELOPMENT INDICATORS

- ONE STORY COMMERCIAL BUILDINGS
- TWO STORY COMMERCIAL BUILDINGS
- VACANT BUILDINGS
- VACANT LAND
- VACANT LAND (OTHER)
- DEVELOPMENT "IN-PLAY"
- C8 ZONES
- DEVELOPMENT CORRIDOR
- CONTEXTUAL / PRESERVATION ZONES
- EXISTING HISTORIC DISTRICTS
- PROPOSED HISTORIC DISTRICTS
- SUBWAY LINE 1
- SUBWAY LINE A
- SUBWAY STATIONS

DEVELOPMENT INDICATORS

GOAL
4

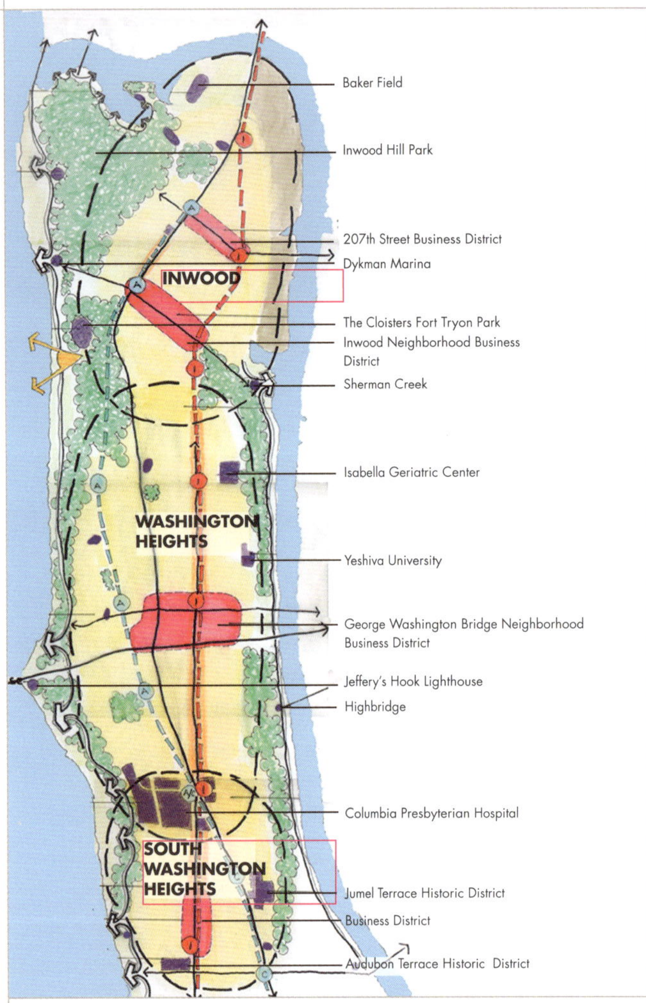

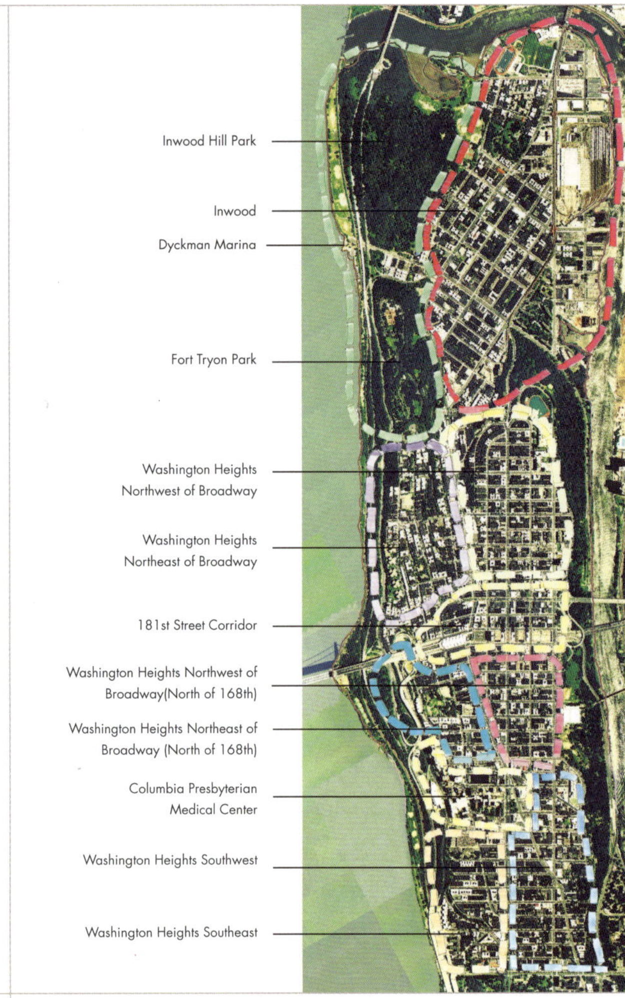

COMMUNITY DISTRICT 12 M

COMMERCIAL AND INTITUTIONAL HUBS

WALKABLE NEIGHBORHOODS

a. PROPOSED WADSWORTH TERRACE DISTRICT

b. AUDUBON PARK & AUDUBON PARK EXTENSION

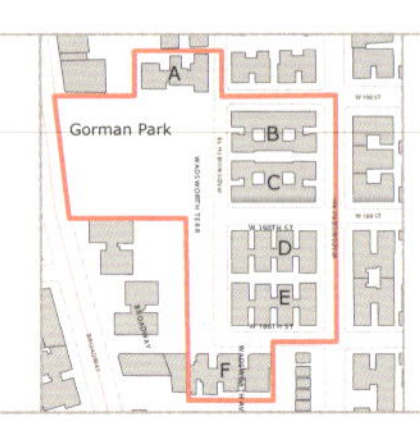

a

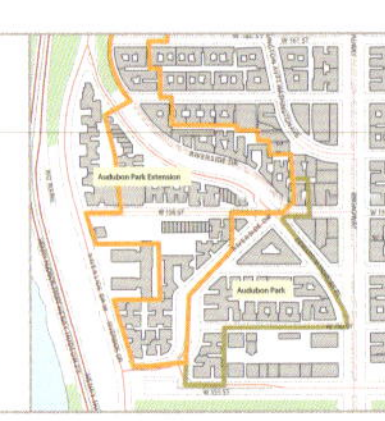

b

GOAL
5

EXISTING HISTORIC CONTEXT

- AUDUBON TERRACE
- JUMEL TERRACE
- HAMILTON HEIGHTS / SUGAR HILL NORTHEAST
- HAMILTON HEIGHTS / SUGAR HILL NORTHWEST
- SCENIC LANDMARK: FORT TRYON PARK
- LPC LANDMARKS

PROPOSED ADDITIONS

PROPOSED HISTORIC DISTRICTS

- AUDUBON PARK
- AUDUBON PARK EXTENSION
- WADSWORTH TERRACE
- PARK TERRACE DISTRICT
- ART DECO SURVEYS: COLUMBIA HISTORIC PRESERVATION PROGRAM & NOMA ART DECO PROYECT (AUDUBON PARTNERSHIP)
- HISTORIC EXPLORATION AREAS (HEA)
- PROPOSED SCENIC LANDMARKS
- PROPOSED ADDITIONS
- NATIONAL & STATE REGISTER

STREETSCAPE ELEMENTS

- PLAQUES
- TREES
- STEPPED STREETS
- HISTORIC LANDMARK LAMPPOSTS

COMMUNITY DISTRICT 12 M

COMPOSITE VIEW

GOAL 6

ZONING

W184TH STREET & OVERLOOK TERRACE CASE STUDY

OPTION 1
QUALITY HOUSING

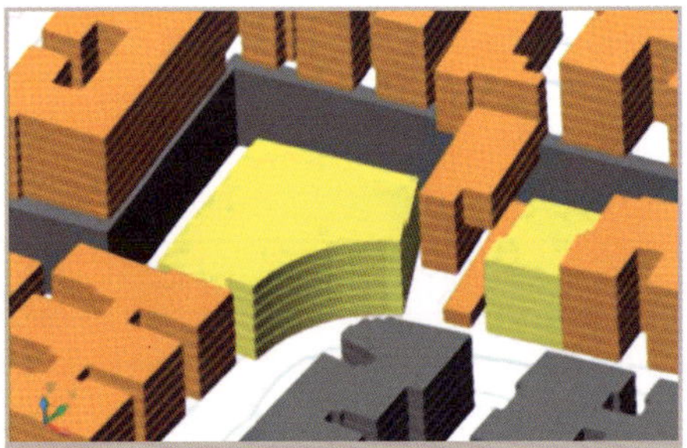

Zoning District	R7: General Residential District	
	R7-2	
Use	Medium Density Apartment Houses	
Remarks	Maximum Residential Floor Area	
	Maximum Lot Coverage	
	Quality Housing	
Maximum FAR (Residential Buildings)	**3.44**	
Floor Area (sf)	127,430	
Required Parking (Off-Street Parking)	50% of total dwelling units	
OSR (minimum)	15.5 - 22.0	
Yard Requirements (ft.)	Front Yard:	None
	Side Yard:	None
	Rear Yard:	20
Setbacks (ft.)	After 60 feet:	30
Height (ft.)	6 stories	

OPTION 2
MAX FAR, MAX HF, MAX OSR

Zoning District	R7: General Residential District	
	R7-2	
Use	Medium Density Apartment Houses	
Remarks	Maximum Residential Floor Area	
	Maximum Lot Coverage	
	Quality Housing	
Maximum FAR (Residential Buildings)	**3.44**	
Floor Area (sf)	127,430	
Required Parking (Off-Street Parking)	50% of total dwelling units	
OSR (minimum)	15.5 - 22.0	
Yard Requirements (ft.)	Front Yard:	None
	Side Yard:	None
	Rear Yard:	20
Setbacks (ft.)	After 60 feet:	30
Height (ft.)	16 stories	

OPTION 3
COMMUNITY FACILITIES

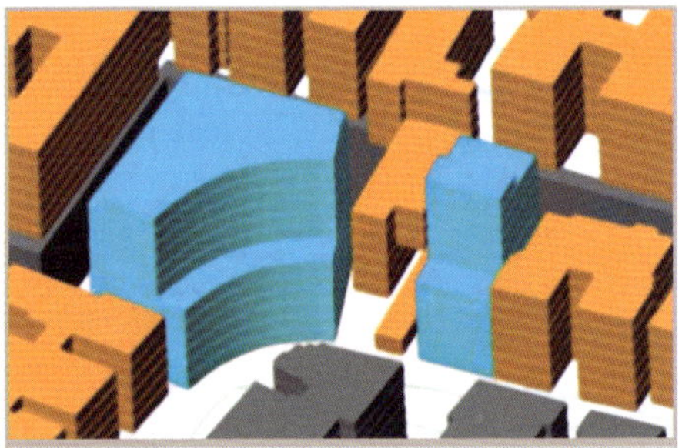

Zoning District	R7: General Residential District	
	R7-2	
Use	Medium Density Apartment Houses	
Remarks	Maximum Residential Floor Area	
	Maximum Lot Coverage	
	Medium Open Space Ratio	
Maximum FAR (Residential Buildings)	**6.5**	
Floor Area (sf)	127,430	
Required Parking (Off-Street Parking)	50% of total dwelling units	
OSR (minimum)	22.0	
Yard Requirements (ft.)	Front Yard:	None
	Side Yard:	None
	Rear Yard:	20
Setbacks (ft.)	After 60 feet:	30
Height (ft.)	12 stories	

COMMUNITY DISTRICT 12- M

EXISTING ZONING & PROPOSED SHERMAN CREEK ZONING

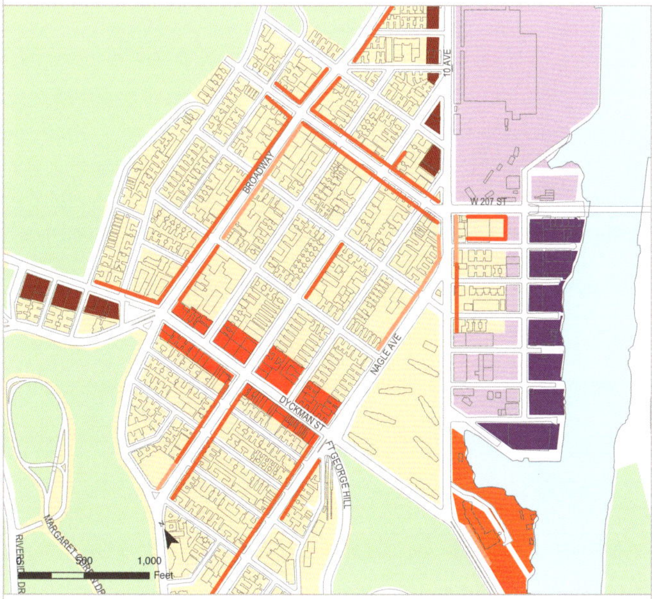

ZONING: EXISTING

	C3	WATERFRONT RECREATION
	C4-4	GENERAL COMMERCIAL
	C8-3	GENERAL SERVICE
	M1-1	LIGHT MANUFACTURING
	M3-1	HEAVY MANUFACTURING
	R7-2	GENERAL RESIDENTIAL
	R8	GENERAL RESIDENTIAL

COMMERCIAL OVERLAY

C1-3

C1-4

C2-1

C2-4

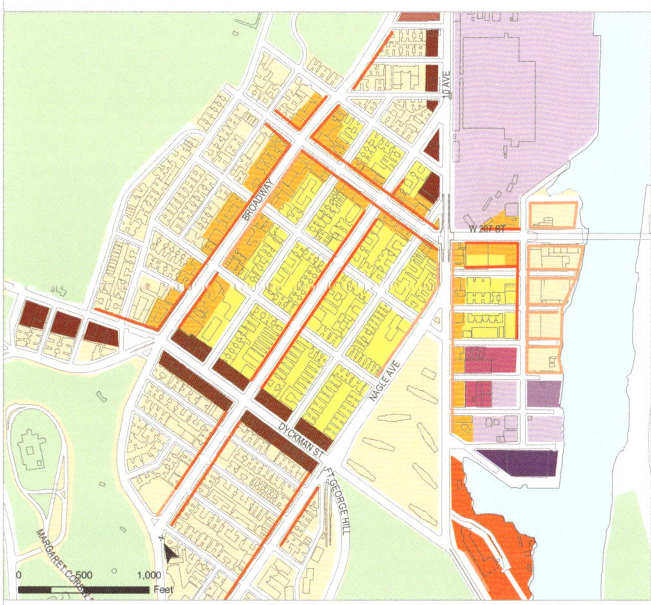

ZONING: PROPOSED

	C3	WATERFRONT RECREATION
	C4-4D	GENERAL COMMERCIAL
	C8-3	GENERAL SERVICE
	M1-1	LIGHT MANUFACTURING
	M1-1/R7-2	MIXED DISTRICT
	M1-1/R7-A	MIXED DISTRICT
	M3-1	HEAVY MANUFACTURING
	R7-2	GENERAL RESIDENTIAL
	R7A	GENERAL RESIDENTIAL
	R8A	GENERAL RESIDENTIAL

COMMERCIAL OVERLAY

C1-4

C2-4

CHAPTER 04

URBAN DESIGN STUDIES

MALCOLM X BOULEVARD
A STREETSCAPE STUDY IN THE MOUNT MORRIS PARK HISTORIC DISTRICT

CHAPTER 04

PARTNERS:

Mount Morris Park Community Improvement Association.
New York Landmarks Conservancy.
New York City Department of Transportation.
New York State Council on the Arts.
Office of Manhattan Borough President Ruth W. Messinger.
East New York Savings Bank.
Bank of New York.

DATE OF PROJECT:

1994 - 1995

Malcolm X Boulevard, also known by its earlier name, Lenox Avenue, passes through the Mount Morris Park Historic District, which is located between West 118th and West 124th Streets. This broad avenue, divided by a central mall, connects Central Park North (110th Street) with the commercial areas at 116th and 125th Streets and with the cultural district centered on 135th Street. The boulevard continues to 147th Street, where it reaches the edge of the Harlem River. Malcolm X Boulevard is one of two picturesque thoroughfares crossing central Harlem. Restoring this culturally, commercially, and historically important boulevard and the surrounding neighborhood is a complicated task, that requires the mitigation of traffic problems as well as the enhancement of neighborhood preservation efforts.

The Landmarks Conservancy has been especially interested in this area, which was designated as an historic district in 1971 for its important heritage of nineteenth-century row houses and churches. Many of the district's homes are currently undergoing reconstruction to restore their turn-of-the century character while accommodating new residents and adapting to new uses. These improvements are spreading into nearby blocks, as residents there upgrade their homes. The Landmarks Conservancy has worked closely with the Mount Morris Park Community Improvement Association (MMPCIA) and has provided low-interest loans and preservation assistance to many homeowners in the district.

MALCOLM X BLV
LENOX AV

MMPCIA and the Landmarks Conservancy originally requested the CCAC's help in looking closely at the rundown section of Malcolm X Boulevard between 118th and 124th streets, which runs directly through the historic district and is an important part of the community. The CCAC, supported by funds from the East New York Savings Bank and the Bank of New York, was asked to create a vision of what this historic boulevard could and should look like in the future by developing cost-effective ways to improve buildings, roadways, and streetscapes in compliance with landmarks laws.

At the time, the New York City Department of Transportation had already made a proposal for upgrading the boulevard, including the section within the historic district. This initial proposal was analyzed by the CCAC to determine its appropriateness, practicality, and aesthetic qualities. The analysis then became the basis of a counterproposal for the area, developed in consultation with the MMPCIA and the New York Landmarks Conservancy.

The study produced by the CCAC provided historical background, analysis of issues affecting the area, and proposals for improving the area's urban design that could be integrated into the boulevard's reconstruction. For those blocks where Malcolm X Boulevard passes through the Mount Morris Park Historic District, the study recorded, both graphically and in photographs, the existing conditions of structures, street features, and building uses. Current and potential activity generators and pedestrian use of the boulevard were noted as well.

The report suggested a vocabulary for street lighting, benches, and planters that would conform to the historical character of the district. The recommendation for each individual block called for integrating street furniture, sidewalk paving, signage, landscaping, and facilities for the disabled and provided proposals for the treatment of storefronts and residential entrances located along the boulevard. What began as a report expanded into an advocacy exercise in which residents, using technical advice from the CCAC and its partners, helped to shape public works decisions in their community. Many of the recommendations noted in the CCAC study were incorporated in NYCDOT's final proposal for the improvement of Malcolm X Boulevard.

LEGEND

- MALCOLM X BLVD
- COMMERCIAL STRIP
- COMMERCIAL NODE
- CULTURAL NODE
- PARK BOUNDARY
- CULTURAL CONNECTOR
- DEAD ENDS
- STUDY AREA
- SUBWAY
- INSTITUTIONAL

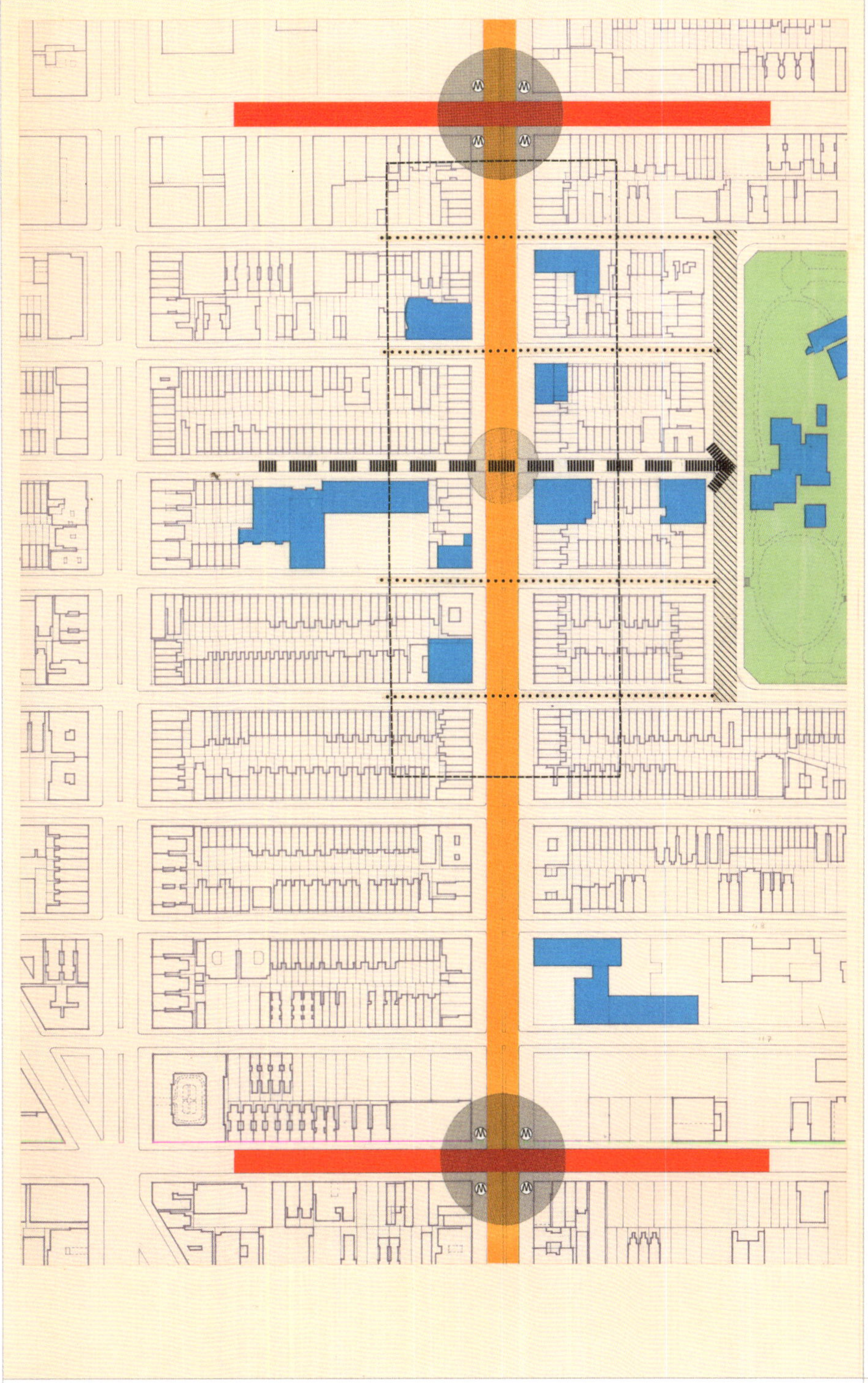

MALCOLM X BOULEVARD

A STREETSCAPE STUDY IN THE MOUNT MORRIS PARK HISTORIC DISTRICT

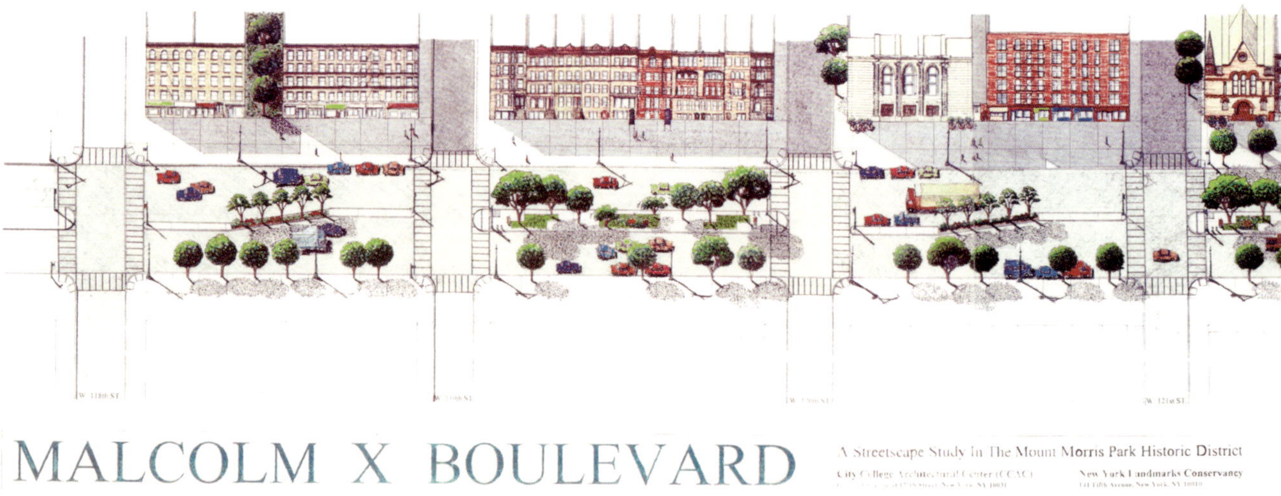

MALCOLM X BOULEVARD

A STREETSCAPE STUDY IN THE MOUNT MORRIS PARK HISTORIC DISTRICT

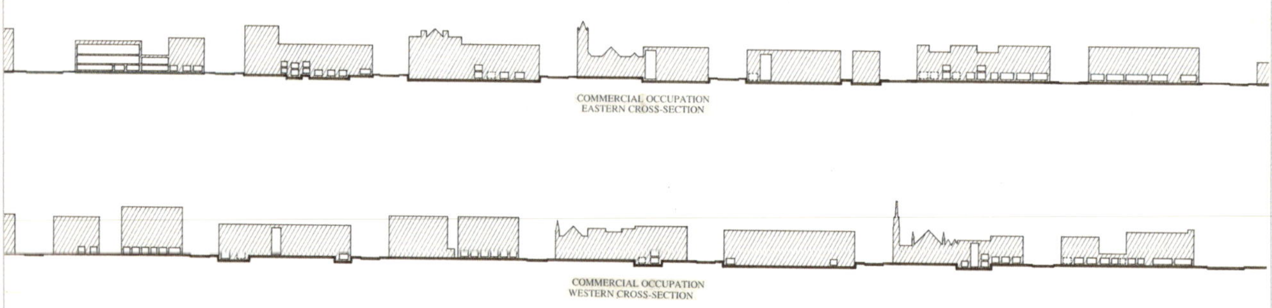

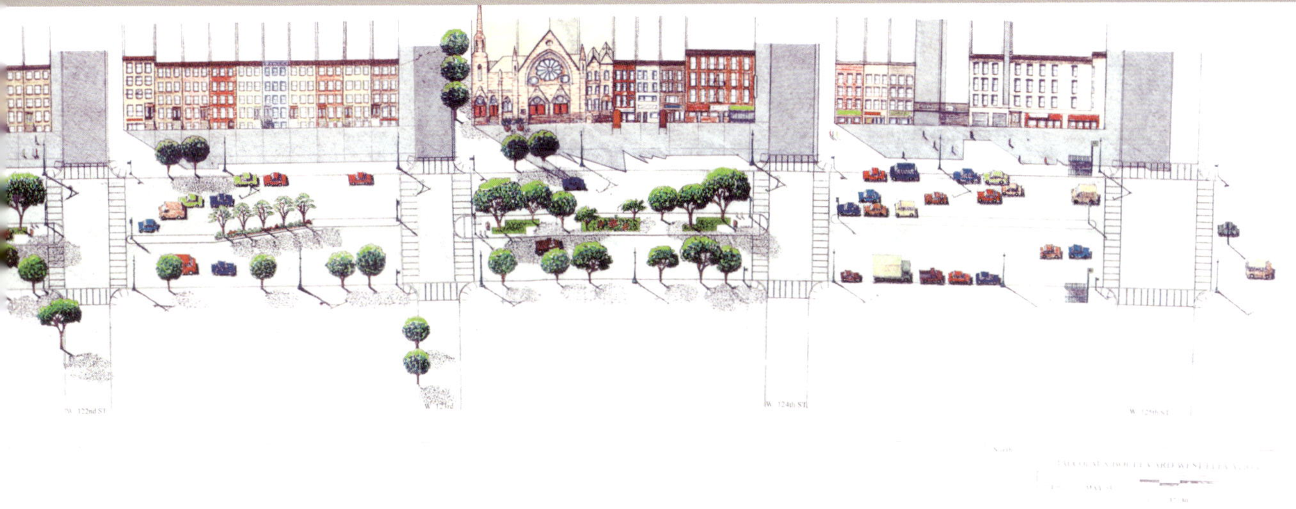

Previous page. Streetscape sections
This page. Streetscape detail

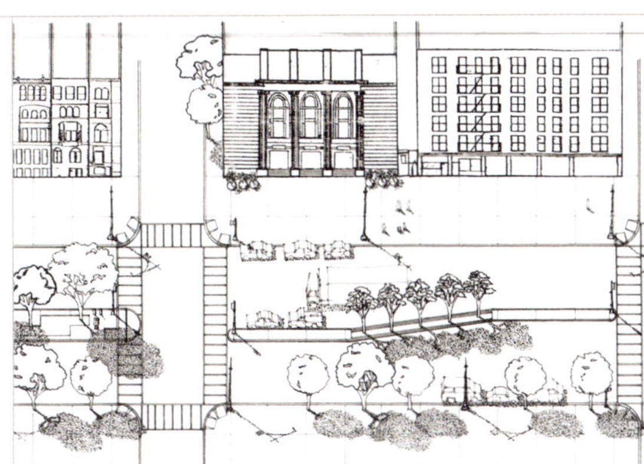

CROSSTOWN 116

CHAPTER 04

PARTNERS:

American Institute of Architects, New York Chapter.
The School of Architecture, Urban Design and Landscape Architecture.
Professor Lance J. Brown.
HUD Office of University Partnerships.
Upper Manhattan Empowerment Zone (UMEZ).

DATE OF PROJECT:

1997

Described by the City College president Yolanda Moses as "a model for how a college should function in relationship to the outside world," Crosstown 116 was a joint project that brought together university students and teachers, local design professionals, and civic groups to envision a new life for 116th Street, a major east-west thoroughfare in upper Manhattan. The project was funded in part by a $109,000 grant from HUD's Office of University Partnerships.

The project's goal was to apply the principles that emerged from the United Nations Conference on Human Settlements (Habitat II), held in Istanbul in 1996, to a real-world situation. The UN conference emphasized the importance of urban design solutions that provide for adequate shelter, community empowerment, sustainability, gender equity, environmental justice, and partnership. The Crosstown 116 participants used these principles to guide them during a year-long design visioning process for the area, which involved four distinct projects:

BRIEFING BOOK
Based on input from a 1996 community event titled "Partnership to Save a City: A Harlem Dialogue," information on the current state of the 116th Street corridor was collected, compiled into a briefing book, and disseminated to local residents and organizations, schools and libraries, agencies, and project participants. Copies were available for review by the public through the three local Community Planning Boards (CPB 9, 10, and 11).

The briefing book provided a common understanding of existing conditions and constraints for subsequent work

on the corridor by local citizens, architects, urban planners, landscape architects, and CCNY and Columbia design students.

DESIGN DIALOGUE

Project organizers held a day-long design charrette and community dialogue, bringing together academics and students, professionals, and community members (the "civic triumvirate") to work collaboratively in teams to explore four topics of concern for the area: (1) providing performance facilities that would enhance local cultural life; (2) the reinvention of public housing; (3) exploring the form of the street and its role as community amenity/ organizer; and (4) looking at the structure of the community and issues of cultural preservation.

SEMINAR SERIES

The CCAC initiated weekly discussions on critical issues in community-building in the area, involving community members, students and faculty, planners and architects and the general public. More than thirty speakers addressed issues such as affordable housing, transportation, and energy-saving design.

DESIGN STUDIOS

The Crosstown 116 project tested a unique idea about how to involve design students in their communities. For the first time, the entire CCNY School of Architecture and Environmental Studies devoted its energies to a single site, and during the school year, all sixteen of CCNY's architecture and urban landscape studios studied the corridor. Ultimately, four teams were formed of CCNY and Columbia University students and local professionals, each charged with creating its own vision for 116th Street as a model twenty-first century urban thoroughfare.

At the end of the Crosstown 116 project, an exhibition was held at CCNY to showcase photographs, drawings, models and texts of concepts and the four different proposals for revitalizing 116th Street. The teams gave a formal presentation of their work to local professionals, leaders, and community members, highlighting different solutions for improving the corridor, including:

1. Reactivating "lost" space around postwar public housing by reintegrating outdoor activities into the city fabric.

2. Finding ways of reinforcing 116th Street's connections to the east and west sides of Morningside Park.

3. Encouraging commercial development near the East River and creating a new node of public-use buildings between Fifth and Lenox avenues.

4. Embedding performance spaces in the center of existing blocks adjacent to 116th Street.

Later that same month, a symposium was held at the United Nations to showcase the participants' work and integrate it into the international context of Habitat II.

Ultimately, the Crosstown 116 project generated a wide range of activities in the local universities and communities. It led the way in creating housing that meets initiative standards; establishing community-based design studio projects; providing project materials for teacher training and high school programs; and forming additional university-community urban design and architectural collaborations, ultimately strengthening ties between the university and the local community it serves.

In 2009, ten years after the project was presented, Carlton Brown, a Crosstown 116 participant and one of the most significant Harlem-based developers of sustainable and affordable properties noted "As a starting point [the] Crosstown 116th Street community design [project] and charrette which grew out of Habitat II influenced our thinking about the work we have since done on 116th Street".

IMAGES OF 116th

There are two sides of 116th street; the Columbia University side of the "other" America and the next side with its Afro-American and immigrant traditions. Both sides are divided by a wall, an empty park, mistrust and fear. Between Morningside Ave. and East River the street seems in perpetual transition. The present confluence of cultures only adds another layer to a rich tradition of immigrant history. Italians, Jews, Puerto Ricans, Mexicans and other nationalities have all added bricks to the images of the street, doing this alongside African-Americans, who seem to remain while other ethnic groups come and go.
The signage of the street reflects ethnic diversity. West Africans represent one of the newest, if not the newest, set of immigrants whose cultures and traditions add to this rich tapestry.
Selling rich fabrics and a variety of crafts, West Africans from Mali, Senegal, Gambia, Nigeria, and other countries bring with them their religion (mainly Islam), music and food.

CROSSTOWN 116

AIA NEW YORK CHAPTER
CCNY SAES

Upper Manhattan Partnership

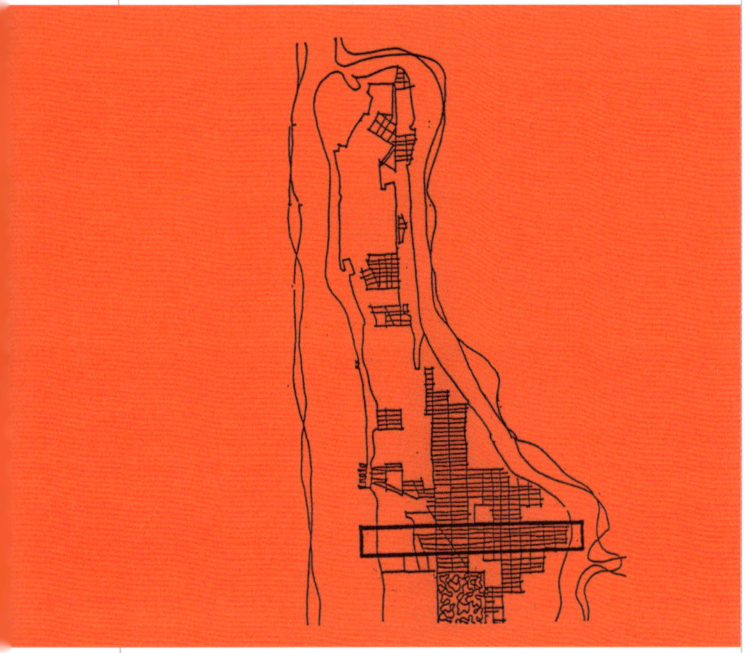

Next page. Program

CROSSTOWN 116 was inspired by the principles of the 1996 United Nations Conference on Human Settlements, HABITAT II. Crosstown 116 creates a "civic triumvirate" between design professionals, design students and community organizations with an interest in the future development of the built environment. CROSSTOWN 116 is a partnership between the AIA New York Chapter, City College of New York School of Architecture and Environmental Studies (SAES) and community organizations in Upper Manhattan. This lecture series is sponsored by the City College of New York School of Architecture andEnvironmental Studies (SAES).

AIA New York Chapter/CCNY-SAES/Upper Manhattan Partnership

CROSSTOWN 116: Bringing Habitat II Home, from Istanbul to Harlem

CITY COLLEGE OF NEW YORK SCHOOL OF ARCHITECTURE AND ENVIRONMENTAL STUDIES

FALL 1997 SEMINAR SERIES

THURSDAY EVENINGS AT 5:45 PM

Shepard Hall, Room 250, 140th Street & Convent Avenue

IRT 1/9 to 137th Street or IND A or D to 145th Street. Call 212.650.8745 for information

9/11 Dialogue I: **UN HABITAT II AGENDA**

Aliye Celik, United Nations Centre for Human Settlements; **Ethel Velez**, James Weldon Johnson Houses Tenants Association

9/18 Dialogue II: **COMMUNITY ISSUES**

Carlton Brown, Full Spectrum Building and Development Corporation; **James H. Carr**, Vice President, Fannie Mae Foundation; **Lionel MacIntyre**, Director, Graduate Program in Urban Planning and Urban Technical Assistance Project, Columbia University

9/25 Dialogue III: **SUSTAINABILITY**

Joyce Lee, Assistant Chief Architect, NYC Office of Management & Budget; Chair, AIA Committee on the Environment; **Peggy Shepard**, Director, West Harlem Environmental Action Coalition

10/9 Dialogue IV: **DEVELOPMENT PROCESS**

Denise A. Hall, AIA, D.A. Hall, Architect; Chair, AIA Women in Architecture Committee; **Alex Saavedra**, Program Associate, Upper Manhattan Empowerment Zone Development Corporation; **Fernando Salicrup**, Director, Puerto Rican Workshop; Julia de Burgos Latino Cultural Center; **Graham Shane**, Ph.D., Professor, Graduate Program in Urban Design, Columbia University

10/16 Dialogue V: **HOUSING ALTERNATIVES**

Karen Franck, New Jersey Institute of Technology; **Beth Greenberg**, AIA, Senior Associate, Richard Dattner Architects; Chair, AIA Housing Committee; **Everardo Agosto Jefferson**, AIA, Principal, Caples Jefferson Architects; Chair, AIA Minority Resources in Architecture Committee

10/23 Dialogue VI: **MIXED USE DEVELOPMENT**

Eddie Baca, Executive Director, Local Development Corporation del Barrio; **Colin Cathcart**, RA, Adjunct Professor, CCNY School of Architecture and Environmental Studies

10/30 Lecture I: **NYC HOUSING TYPOLOGY**

Carmi Bee, FAIA, Professor, CCNY School of Architecture and Environmental Studies

11/6 Dialogue VII: **TRANSPORTATION ISSUES**

Staff representative, Regional Plan Association; Committee representative, AIA Transportation & Infrastructure Committee; **Shampa Chanda**, APA, NYC Department of Transportation

11/13 Lecture II: **HOUSING PROTOTYPES STUDY**

Michael Kwartler, FAIA, Director, New School Environmental Simulation Laboratory; **Petr Stand**, APA, Magnusson Architecture & Planning

11/25 Dialogue VIII: **AFFORDABLE HOUSING**

David Burney, Director, Design and Capital Improvement, New York City Housing Authority Representative, AIA Housing Committee; **Stephen A. Campbell**, R.A., Phoenix Design

Poster design by Tana Bigelow and Marilyn Gallagher

CROSSTOWN 116

LAND USE MAP

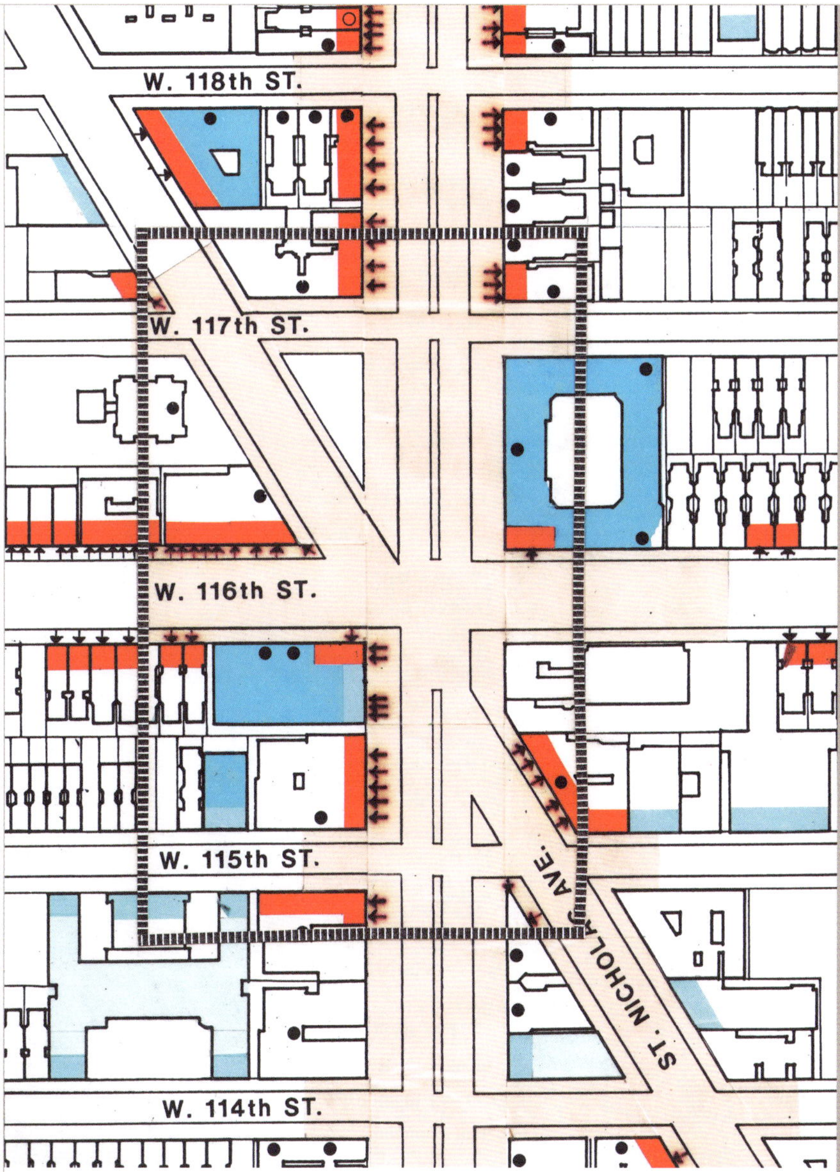

CROSSTOWN 116

AIA NEW YORK CHAPTER / CCNY / UPPER MANHATTAN PARTNERSHIP

This page. A. Philip Randolph Square

DISCOVERING THE CENTER: A VISION PLAN FOR THE BRONX HUB

CHAPTER 04

PARTNERS:

American Institute of Architects New York Chapter.
Bronx Borough President Fernando Ferrer and Staff.
Bronx Community Board 1.
New York National Bank.
Nos Quedamos.
Bernd Zimmermann, Bronx Planning and Development.
South Bronx Overall Economic Development Corporation.

DATE OF PROJECT:

2000 - 2001

The CCAC collaborated with community development organizations and the office of the Bronx borough president to generate a vision plan for the Hub at East 149th Street and Third Avenue, the historic transportation and commercial nexus of the South Bronx.

The Hub has more than one identity in the minds of Bronx residents. For many, it is the central transit connection in the borough, the crossroads where Third, Willis, and Melrose avenues and East 149th Street come together. At this spot, where the Third Avenue El once terminated, many bus routes serving the Bronx and Manhattan intersect with one another and with the East and West Side subway lines. For some, the Hub refers to the triangular island within the intersection south of 149th Street. Officially named Roberto Clemente Plaza, this "Times Square" of the Bronx was created from the leftover space formed by the convergence of important thoroughfares. Others think of the Hub as the downtown business district of the Bronx, one that naturally grew up around this crossroads, serving not only the adjacent neighborhoods but also residents farther away who can easily reach the Hub through the transportation network.

Part of the visioning task was to refine the geographic boundaries of the study area and more accurately define the identity of the Hub as a unique place or district. The CCAC began looking at a roughly sixty-block area bounded by Park Avenue to the west, St. Ann's to the east, East 146th Street to the south, and East 156th Street to the north. In offering proposals for the revitalization of the Hub, the CCAC identified certain locations as thresholds or gateways from the surrounding residential or institutional areas into the commercial core of this downtown area.

YOUR FURNITURE STOP
YOUR FURNITURE STOP
GALLERY ORO
FINE JEWELRY & WATCHES
GALLERY ORO
2000
FINE JEWELRY & WATCHES
SPECIAL ORDERS
EXPERT REPAIR
OPEN SUNDAYS
BEEP
BEEP 2000
ONE WAY

While current zoning codifies these historic distinctions, measures that reinforce the sense of an inner commercial district will be needed to encourage the growth and vitality of this area.

The CCAC, with the help of faculty and students from City College, conducted a study documenting the area through maps and inventories of features such as buildings, transit routes, and vacant lots. Borough president Fernando Ferrer and his staff, under the direction of Bronx planning and development director Bernd Zimmermann, facilitated a series of meetings with community and government stakeholders with interests in the Hub area. New York National Bank, headquartered on East 149th Street, took the lead in raising money from banks with branches in the area for the study.

Three initial meetings took place, acting as separate forums addressing different constituencies: the first was held with city agencies, not-for-profit developers, and a commercial developer with projects pending for the Hub; the second with owners of businesses and commercial properties in the area; and the third with residents of surrounding neighborhoods, including representatives from Bronx Community Board 1. Concerns were raised and recommendations given regarding pedestrian and traffic safety and plans for rebuilding the major streets that run through the Hub. Also put forward were requests for proposals to develop the large parcels of vacant land in the area, as well as proposals for bus circulation and the conception of the Hub as an intermodal transfer node. The CCAC team then met with community representatives and residents in public forums to present the progress of its research and test assumptions. The feedback gained from these meetings proved very helpful toward developing strategies for diverse issues such as land use, public transportation, traffic mitigation, and street planning.

The CCAC marshaled the resources of City College to carry out this study. Eight students from the Architecture, Urban Design, and Landscape Architecture programs participated in the project. They collected data for the inventory and site analysis of the area, developed design proposals in drawings and models, and presented the work in progress to meetings of community representatives.

After the research and input phases of the project, the CCAC issued Discovering the Center: A Vision Plan for the Bronx Hub, a report assessing the critical challenges and opportunities for the revitalization and long-term viability of the Hub as an important center of commercial, civic, and cultural activity. The plan's recommendations addressed specific issues such as public transit, traffic calming, pedestrian improvements, architectural preservation, zoning, and guidelines for developing vacant parcels. The plan sought to offer strategies to ease transportation conflicts, to foster a sustainable mix of activities necessary for a healthy downtown, to improve the public-space environment, and to reveal the architectural character of existing commercial buildings while proposing new development that would reestablish the physical density and proximity of uses one finds in a vital downtown core. This project was intended to become a model for future work by the CCAC, in the breadth of issues considered, the process of engaging stakeholders, and the attention given to preserving the area's historic character and significance as an active downtown center.

The area is now host to several new development initiatives suggested by the report. A large-scale commercial complex is complemented by Via Verde, a new green housing and community center project that was spawned through the New Housing New York competition sponsored by the New York chapter of the American Institute of Architects.

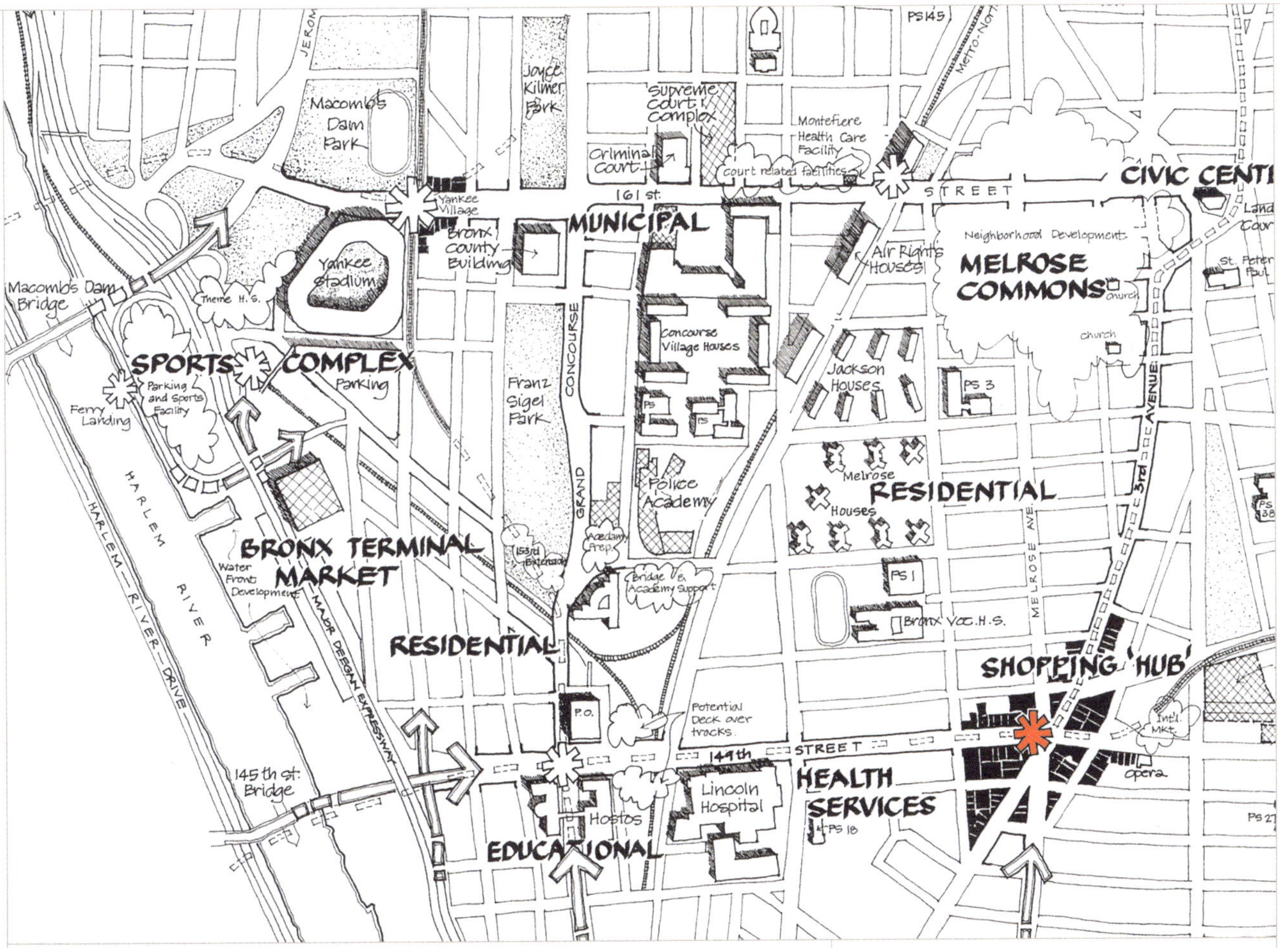

BRONX CENTER MAP

Aerial Photo

a

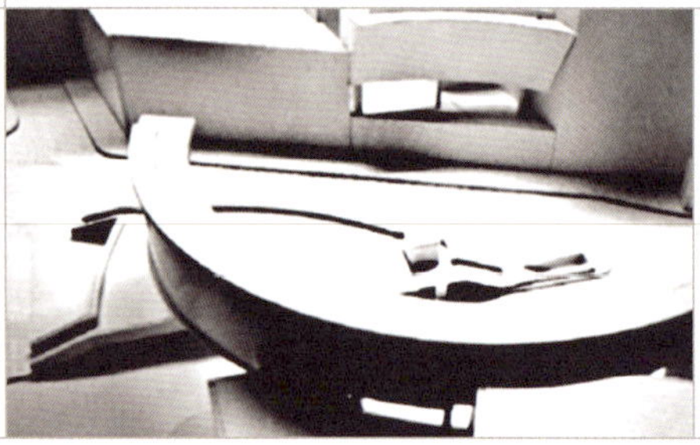

b

a and c. Bronx Hub Plan Drowing
c. Bronx Hub Model
d. Bronx Hub

c

d

138TH STREET CORRIDOR, THE BRONX

CHAPTER 04

PARTNERS:

South Bronx Overall Economic Development Corporation.
CUNY Institute for UrbanSystems.
138th Street Merchants and Professionals Association.

DATE OF PROJECT:

2003

The one-and-a-half-mile 138th Street in the Bronx resembles any Main Street in a small city or town; it's the spine that holds disparate areas together and provides a clear identity to the surrounding communities. Sections of 138th Street that pass through neglected industrial areas and across perimeter highways and major thoroughfares pose special challenges to maintaining this important overall sense of identity.

The CCAC was contacted by the South Bronx Overall Economic Development Corporation (SoBRO) to develop concept ideas as the first phase of streetscape revitalization. The resulting plan for 138th Street aimed to provide a framework to help SoBRO, the community, and city agencies identify priorities for enhancing the cohesion of this corridor and undertake new projects for its improvement.

Like any major corridor, 138th Street is composed of different zones; the challenge is to mold this diverse environment into an interrelated unit. The study's urban-design recommendations were intended to contribute to a cohesive streetscape that would unify the environment. Because each zone has its own needs, constraints, and constituencies, the CCAC study recognized that different partnerships would need to form to implement the overall strategy within each specific area.

In the commercial core, between Alexander and Cypress avenues, the plan suggested focusing on the building fronts—store windows, merchandise display, signage, and entrances—to upgrade them and make them more cohesive. Capital improvements, including new sidewalks, curbs, and more attractive and more frequently spaced lighting, would also help to improve the appearance,

12'-11"
CLEARANCE
ALL NATURAL
Snapple

functionality, and safety of the street. In addition, "No Through Trucks" restrictions would help decrease the area's chronic traffic congestion problems.

The area from Lincoln to Alexander avenues is an assemblage of a police station, a library, a church, public housing, and small shops. These blocks function as the civic center and institutional hub of the corridor. The plan suggested enhancing the civic character of this area through careful public-space design and creation of an outdoor market.

In other key areas, especially the Gateway (at the beginning of the Grand Concourse), the Crossroads (where Third, Morris, and Lincoln avenues intersect), and the Bruckner portal (the gateway at the east end of 138th Street), significant design and capital investment in public spaces were suggested to help spur interest in private development. SoBRO has taken many of the CCAC's recommendations and is rebuilding much of the dilapidated building stock.

a

a. Sketch Gateway
b. Sketch Gateway Reverse

b

CONCEPT PLAN

138TH STREET

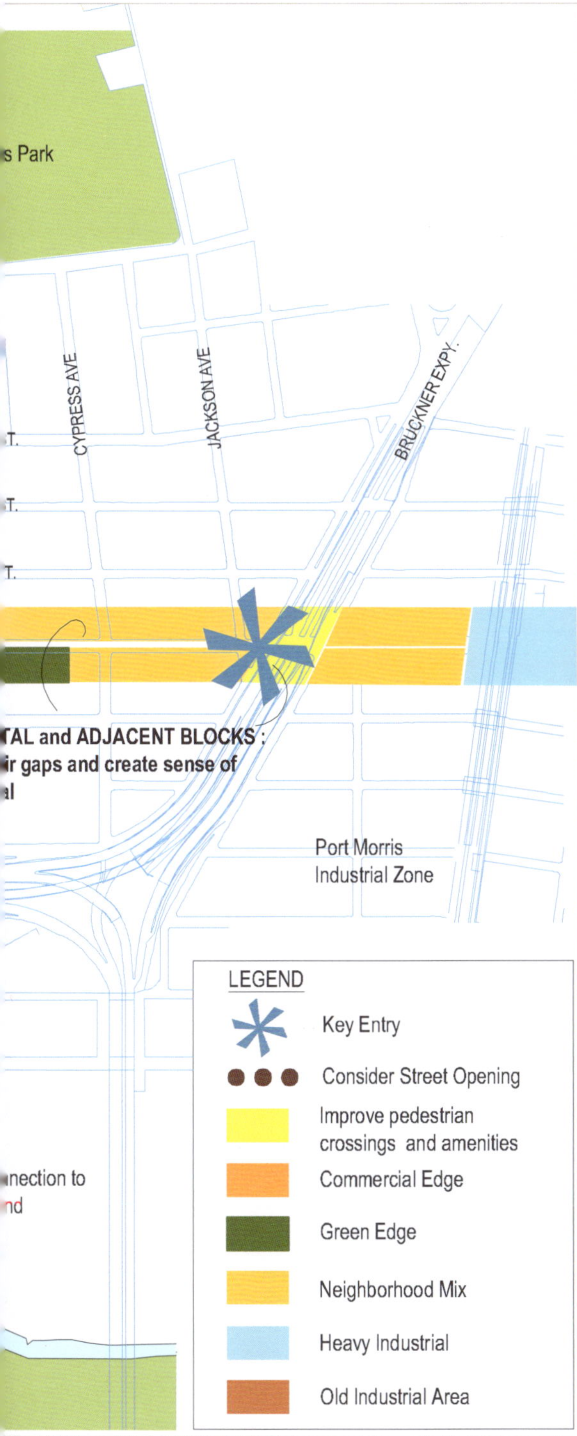

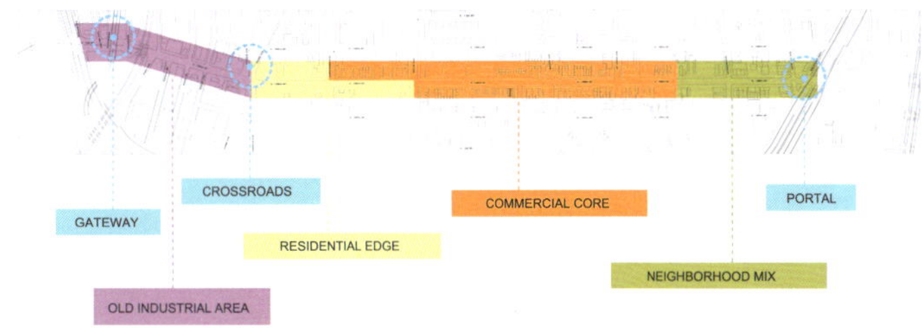

ZONE DIAGRAM

138TH STREET

BLOCK 1

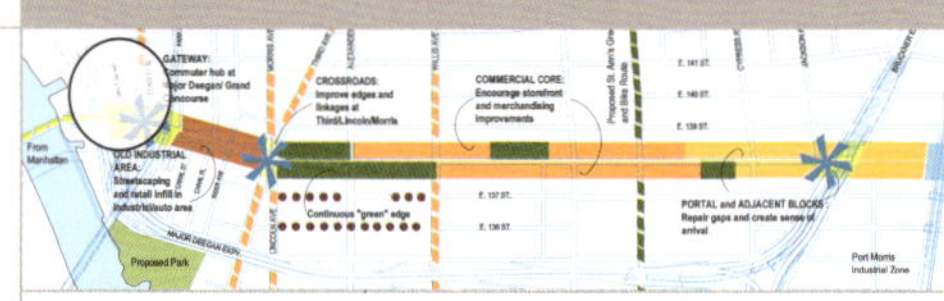

LOCATION OF BLOCK 1

IN THE OVERALL PLAN

BLOCK 2

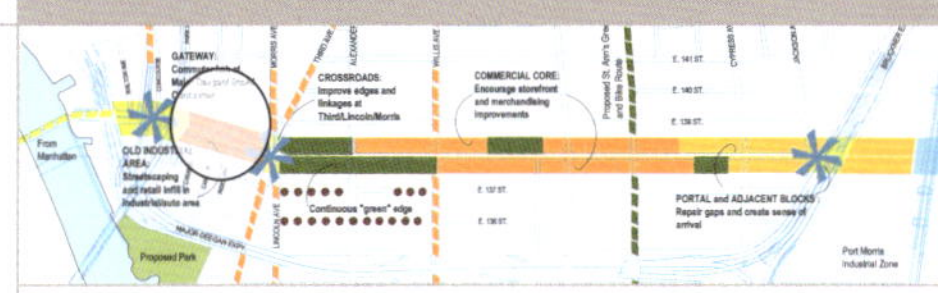

LOCATION OF BLOCK 2

IN THE OVERALL PLAN

Sketch. Industrial Area

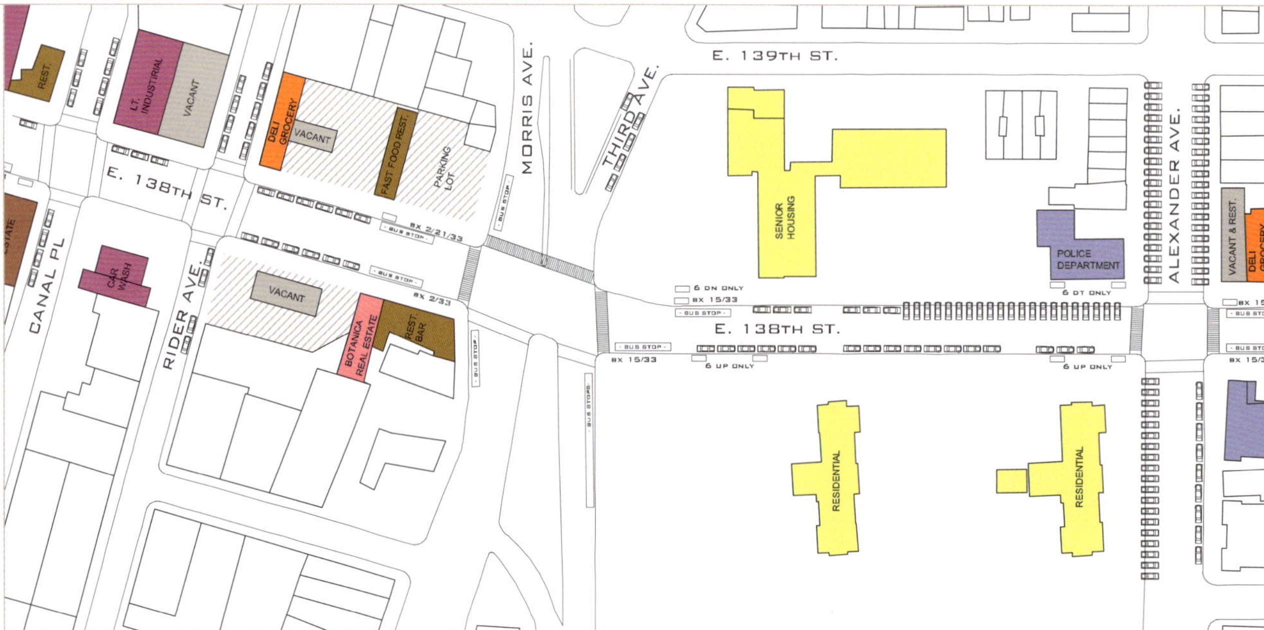

BLOCK 3

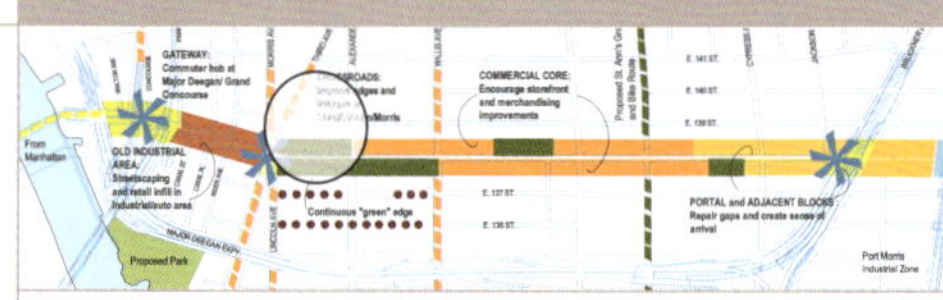

LOCATION OF BLOCK 3

IN THE OVERALL PLAN

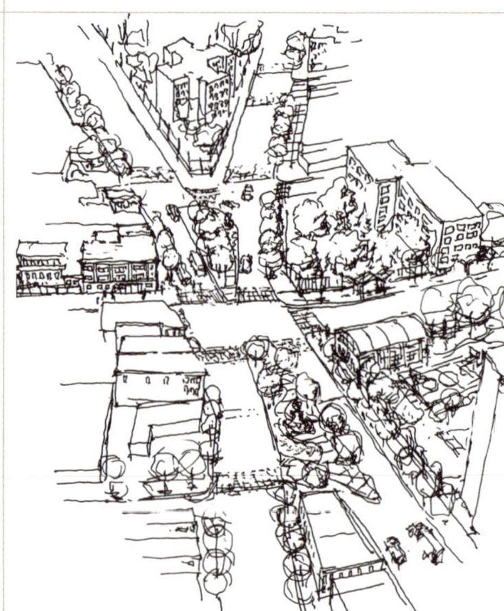

Sketch. Crossroad

BLOCK 4

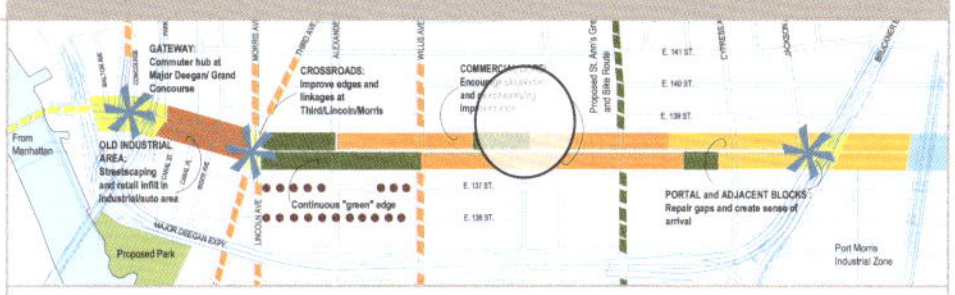

LOCATION OF BLOCK 4

IN THE OVERALL PLAN

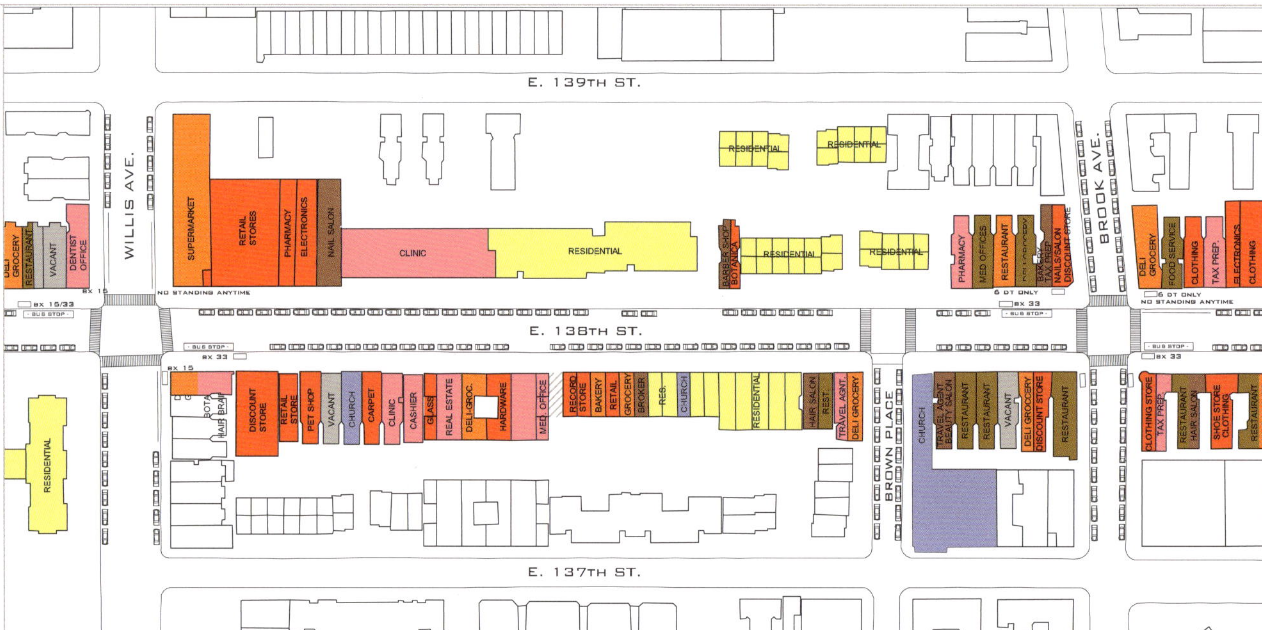

BLOCK 5

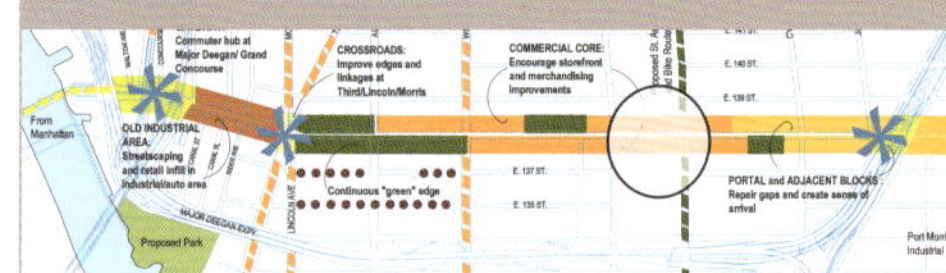

LOCATION OF BLOCK 5

IN THE OVERALL PLAN

Sketch. Market

BLOCK 6

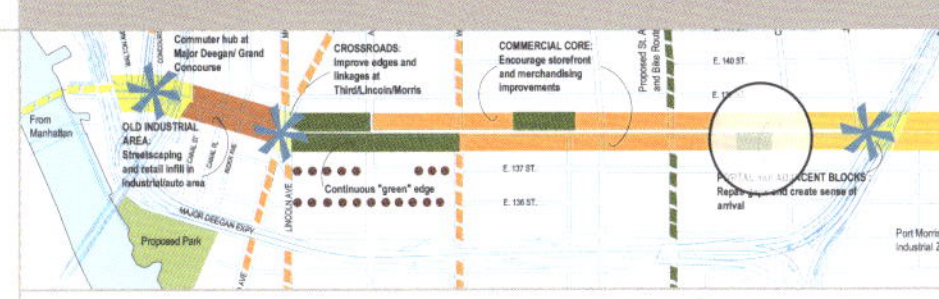

LOCATION OF BLOCK 6

IN THE OVERALL PLAN

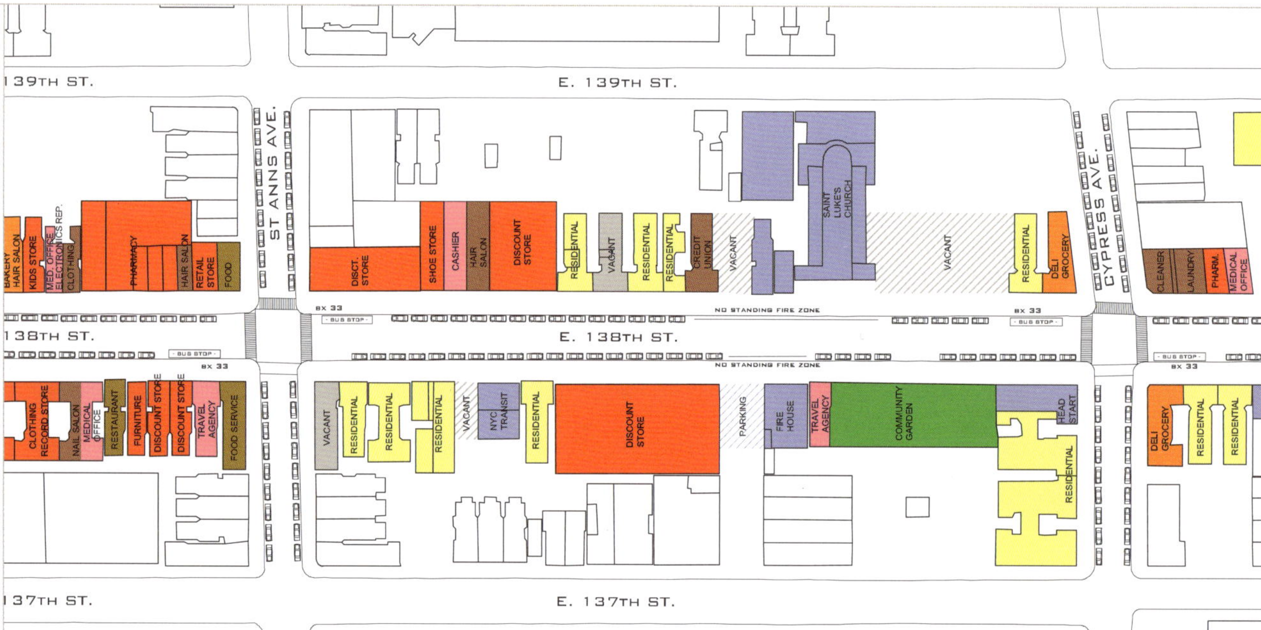

BLOCK 7

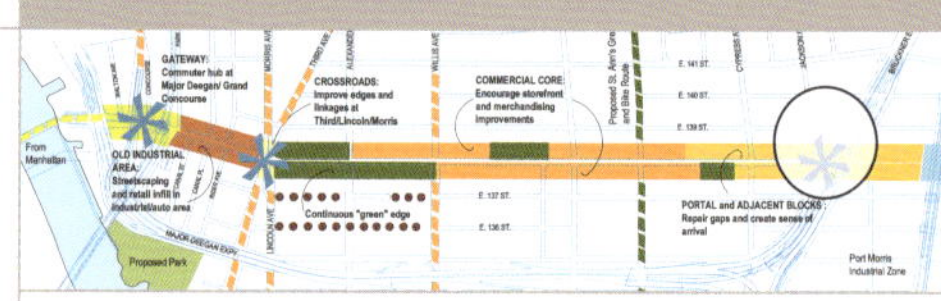

LOCATION OF BLOCK 7

IN THE OVERALL PLAN

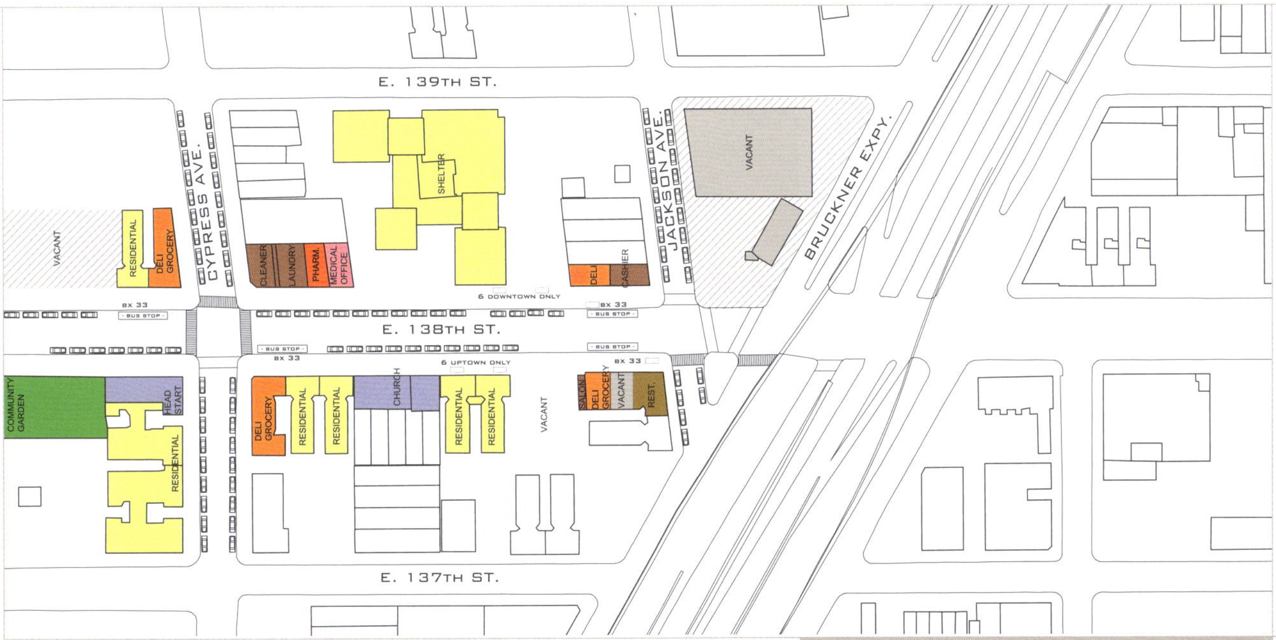

BLOCK 8

LOCATION OF BLOCK 8

IN THE OVERALL PLAN

MOUNT VERNON ACTION PLAN

CHAPTER 04

PARTNERS:

City of Mount Vernon.
State of New York Division of Coastal Resources.

DATE OF PROJECT:

2002 - 2008

In 2002, the Mount Vernon Urban Renewal Agency created a City Center Improvement Plan with the intention of revitalizing Mount Vernon's central business district. The CCAC was asked to prepare a report to assist the city's effort.

In 2003, the CCAC presented its report, Analysis and Recommendations for the Central Business District. The study detailed existing conditions, land use, and community priorities, as well as recommending improvements to storefronts and building design alternatives for pocket parks and open spaces.

In 2006, Mount Vernon received a Quality Communities Grant from the Division of Coastal Resources to revise the existing report and prepare a new report. This report, Downtown Action Plan for the City, updated the previous analysis of existing conditions and proposed additional possibilities for future revitalization of the downtown central business district. Recommendations took into account the new three-phase plan for re-zoning for higher density housing, exposing the positive effects of the re-zoning on the commercial corridors and development around transportation hubs.

Downtown Action Plan for the City identified three issues of paramount importance in the redevelopment strategy for Mount Vernon's central downtown district:

- The need to create employment-generating incubators in the area.

Strengthening local opportunities was identified as a key part of the plan to attract companies and private enterprises. The first step toward this goal was the establishment of job training centers for youth, women, and senior citizens. As Michael Porter stated in "**An Economic Strategy for America's Inner Cities**," "Economic development in inner cities will come only from enhancing the advantages of an inner-city location and building on the base of existing companies." The city's close proximity to Manhattan, its good vehicular connections to Westchester County, and a strong and growing labor base make increased economic development a viable objective.

Actions in support of the creation of employment generators can include the establishment of ESL education programs, language classes, digital literacy programs, paraprofessional and secretarial classes, child care and elderly care certificate courses, and various courses required for jobs in transportation services.

- The importance of emphasizing the restoration and adaptation of existing commercial and residential building stock and integrating mixed-use development in the downtown area.

The building stock in the City of Mount Vernon is well suited to mixed-use development, mixed-income housing, historic resources development, and industrial start-ups. One benefit of this approach is that adaptive re-uses are often less disruptive to the surrounding commercial activities in the area during construction. Previously residential structures that are now in highly commercial districts can be retrofitted for new purposes. These existing buildings are in some cases visual keys for important intersections, and retaining them improves the visibility and legibility of the economic development taking place.

- The importance of instituting sustainable practices as part of the development strategy for the revitalization.

As Mount Vernon works toward improved economic-generator centers and increased density of the downtown district, the city must identify and implement physically and socially sustainable practices. The CCAC report recommends promoting energy-efficient buildings; redundant transportation alternatives; water-quality remediation and the use of permeable surfaces; the reduction of waste and the reuse of materials; and the enhancement of open-space systems and connecting them with the physical and social fabric of the city, including holding programmed events and markets.

The CCAC's action plan delineated several manageable changes and new directions for redeveloping the central core of the City of Mount Vernon that can promote short-term, mid-term, and long-term achievements for strengthening both the commerce and community life of the city. In addition, the CCAC suggested possible funding sources to kick-start the process of revitalization.

Since there are quite a number of financial resources and grant programs that are available to the City of Mount Vernon to implement projects, the city and its residents, and in particular the commercial district stakeholders, need to support and decide upon the priority and the timing of the issues to be addressed as described in the report so the grant application program can begin. The CCAC stressed to city officials the need to understand the strength embodied in civic organizations already in existence. The inclusion of as many residents as possible in the planning process—especially disenfranchised youth and new immigrants, who represent the future of the city—will help in obtaining federal and state assistance.

The plan produced by the CCAC in collaboration with Mayor Davis and his successor, Mayor Young, was accepted by the state director of the New York Division of Coastal Resources and by the staff of the City of Mount Vernon. This plan became the impetus for the creation of a city-wide general plan, which has been approved by the city and the county and has initiated an ongoing process of community participation with the involvement of private developers and municipal professional staff.

LOCATION
MAPS

a

a. Aerial, Mt. Vernon East
b. City Map, Mt. Vernon

REGIONAL MAP
MOUNT VERNON

b

PROPOSAL

- RE-ZONING
- TRANSIT ORIENTED DEVELOPMENT
- SUSTAINABLE PRACTICES
- EMPLOYMENT GENERATION
- FACADE IMPROVEMENT
- ARTS DISTRICT

CENTERS

REZONING

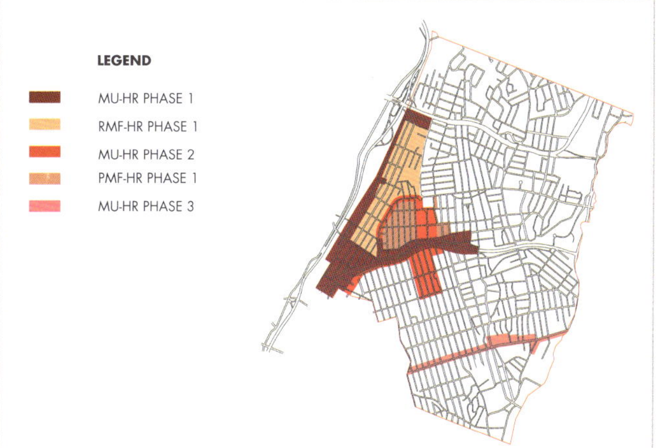

RE-ZONING

Re-zoning sections of Mt. Vernon that are adjacent to public transportation and downtown commercial districts will present the potential for high density mixed-use developments and multi-family high rises, which are essential to the economic vitality of the city. The proposed zoning code is for MU-HR 10 to 15 and RMF-HR 10. These zoning codes will essentially permit developers to build 7 stories or higher in areas that are currently underutilized. Many of the existing structures in this area are comprised of a variety of densities from single family homes, light manufacturing and storage facilities, to a few high rise residential buildings. Re-zoning for higher densities will encourage higher density development, which will reflect upon the urban landscape and population living in Mount Vernon.

MU-HR PHASE 1

TOTAL LAND USE AREA: 5273952

- MULTIPLE FAMILY (162086 SQ.FT.)
- 2-3 FAMILY (490214 SQ. FT.)
- SINGLE FAMILY (101873 SQ. FT.)
- EXISTING (2529268 SQ.FT.)
- INDUSTRIAL (1600704 SQ.FT.)
- RELIGIOUS (6370 SQ.FT.)
- RETAIL / SERVICES (190027 SQ. FT.)
- RESTAURANTS (109253 SQ. FT.)
- THEATERS / HOSTELS (84157 SQ. FT.)

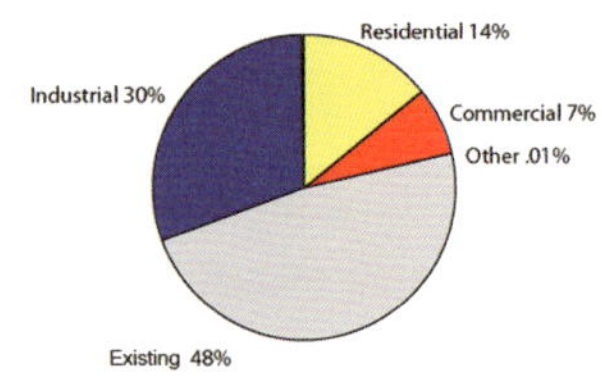

Phase 1, MU-HR:

The western boundary runs north along the rail line and Macquesten Parkway, and is bounded by Cross County Parkway on the north side and a short strip comes east from Macquesten on the south side.

MU-HR PHASE 2

TOTAL LAND USE AREA: 3669574

- MULTIPLE FAMILY (296571 SQ.FT.)
- 2-3 FAMILY (156460 SQ. FT.)
- SINGLE FAMILY (158370 SQ. FT.)
- EXISTING (2529268 SQ.FT.)
- INDUSTRIAL (707772 SQ.FT.)
- RELIGIOUS / CIVIC (57340 SQ.FT.)
- RETAIL / SERVICES (450795 SQ. FT.)
- RESTAURANTS (43258 SQ. FT.)
- THEATERS / HOSTELS (49783 SQ. FT.)

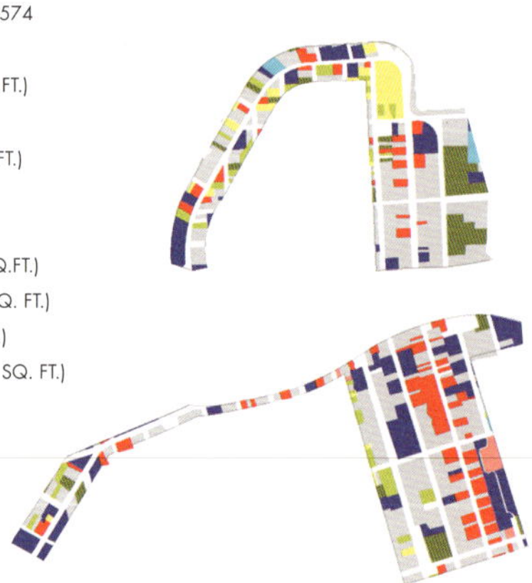

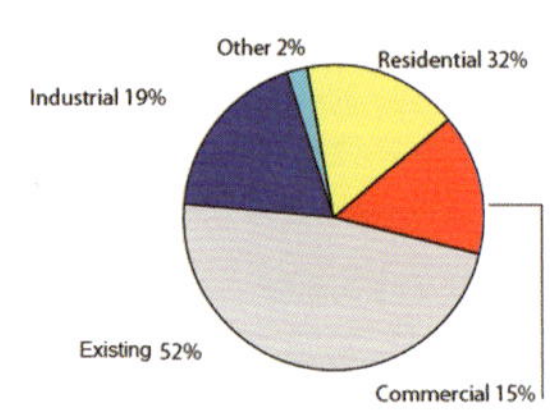

Phase 2, MU-HR:

This area is partitioned into two sections, north and south, by the Phase 1 re-zoning. The northern portion begins at West Lincoln Avenue and Oak Street, and continues along West Lincoln Avenue until it reaches Gramatan Avenue. Here it follows the southwestern edge of Hartley Park, bounded by Gramatan Avenue and North Street. It then turns south at North 2nd Avenue and continues along this line (through the street straight to Prospect Avenue.

MU-HR PHASE 3

TOTAL LAND USE AREA: 1588849

- MULTIPLE FAMILY (19663 SQ.FT.)
- 2-3 FAMILY (98941 SQ. FT.)
- SINGLE FAMILY (42531 SQ. FT.)
- EXISTING (2529268 SQ.FT.)
- INDUSTRIAL (973101 SQ.FT.)
- CIVIC (2869 SQ.FT.)
- RETAIL / SERVICES (72083 SQ. FT.)
- RESTAURANTS (11273 SQ. FT.)
- THEATERS / HOSTELS (49783 SQ. FT.)

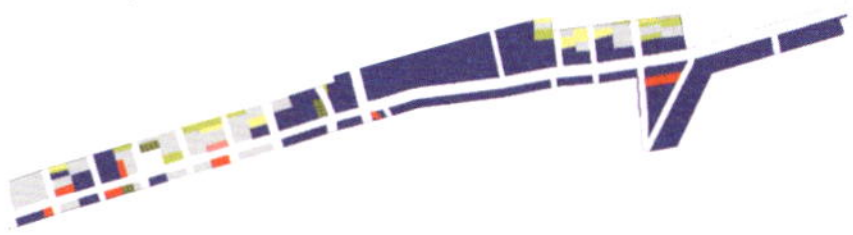

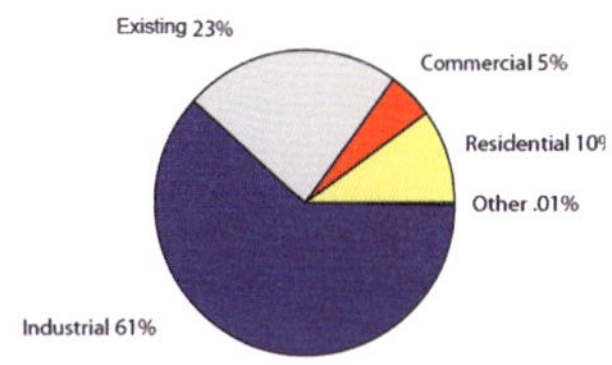

Phase 3, MU-HR:

This area begins at Mundy Lane and Sandford Boulevard and runs east along to the Hutchinson River Parkway South.

RMF-HR PHASE 1

TOTAL LAND USE AREA: 4355690

- MULTIPLE FAMILY (208266 SQ.FT.)
- 2-3 FAMILY (952637 SQ. FT.)
- SINGLE FAMILY (418860 SQ. FT.)
- EXISTING (26661111 SQ.FT.)
- INDUSTRIAL (617323 SQ.FT.)
- RELIGIOUS (12235 SQ.FT.)
- RETAIL / SERVICES (55651 SQ. FT.)
- RESTAURANTS (22849 SQ. FT.)
- THEATERS / HOSTELS (1758 SQ. FT.)

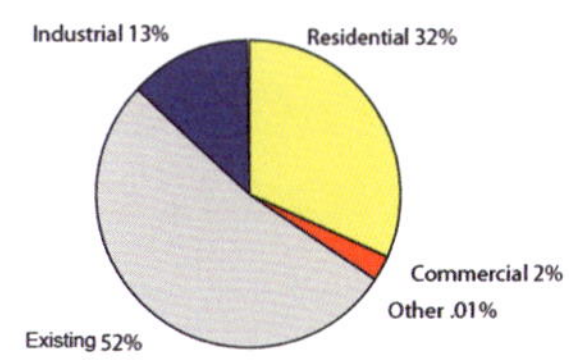

Phase 1, RMF-HR:

This boundary is made by Macquesten Parkway North to the west; West Grand Street to the north; Gramatan Avenue and East Lincoln Avenue to the east; and Mount Vernon Avenue to the south.

RMF-HR PHASE 2

TOTAL LAND USE AREA: 1967647 SQ. FT.

- MULTIPLE FAMILY (153363 SQ.FT.)
- 2-3 FAMILY (552008 SQ. FT.)
- SINGLE FAMILY (144948 SQ. FT.)
- EXISTING (2529268 SQ.FT.)
- INDUSTRIAL (87683 SQ.FT.)
- CIVIC (12092 SQ.FT.)
- RETAIL / SERVICES (17018 SQ. FT.)

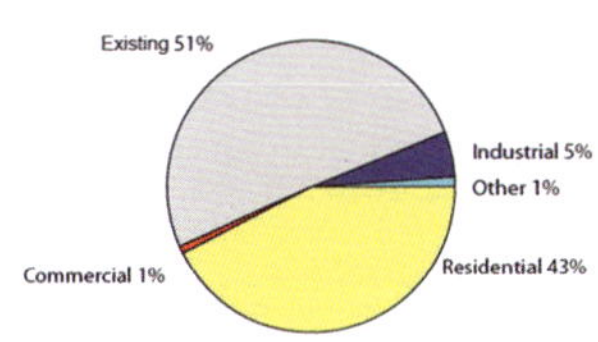

Phase 2, HMF-HR:

This area is partitioned into two sections by the MUHR area of phase development. The western portion is bounded by Prospect Avenue to the south, Sharp Avenue to the east, and Lincoln Avenue to the north and west, excluding the lots facing Lincoln Avenue.

TRANSIT ORIENTED DEVELOPMENT

As Mount Vernon redevelops the area near the Mount Vernon East rail line, it is important to include several options to walk to the train station. These walks may be ramps and staircases between street level and the train station as well as ramps connecting the newly developed mixed-use buildings to the train station. This is an important way to promote interaction with redeveloped commercial space.

Transit oriented development should not minimize vehicular use in favor of pedestrian use and should try and integrate roadways, pedestrian pathways and adequate amounts of parking within the development zones. Currently, Mount Vernon has adequate parking. The key to utilizing the space better is to build municipal parking vertically near the train stations, and integrate parking lots within some mixed-use developments.

Transit oriented development not only informs what types of structures to build, but how to make an area legible to pedestrians and vehicular traffic. Promoting legibility with cross walks and signage, particularly at bridge crossings, will help connect development on either side of the Mount Vernon East rail line. Pedestrians tend to keep to the right on sidewalks, thus right-hand pedestrian flow and sidewalk bulb-outs are recommended for increasing pedestrian flow and traffic calming measures for vehicles.

TRANSIT ORIENTED DEVELOPMENT MAP

SUSTAINABLE PRACTICES

Before

After

GREEN MARKET

An important aspect of planning for sustainability is the concept of initiating long term goals for all projects. Even projects with immediate applicability are considered for their long term investment. Efforts at sustainability should be considered on both local and regional scales, as should the project at hand's positive or negative effects on each scale.. Some sustainable initiatives, (although certainly not limited to these examples) are:

- Walkability and legibility of streetscapes;
- Preservation of open space;
- Water remediation and surface permeability;
- Reduction of waste and the re-use of materials;
- Development of a self-sustaining economy;
- Support of community and local commerce through the promotion of local food sources;
- Energy efficienct practices for buildings.

a. Gramatan Avenue streetscape improvement.
b. East 1st & South 3rd intersection.

Before

After **a** **b**

EMPLOYMENT GENERATION

As Westchester County residents increasingly get older and as the baby boomer generation retires, the need for long-term care and senior citizen facilities becomes a pressing matter. Mount Vernon can strengthen its central business base and increase the pedestrian mobility of the downtown areas by investing in centrally located senior facilities. Training residents as nurses and caretakers can produce a permanent job base for the city of Mount Vernon.
Several suggestions to increase employment generation and economic vitality in Mount Vernon are listed below.

- Job Training
- Youth Centers and Mentoring Programs
- Senior and Long-term Care Facilities

Job center opportunities.

CIRCLES
REGIONAL MAP

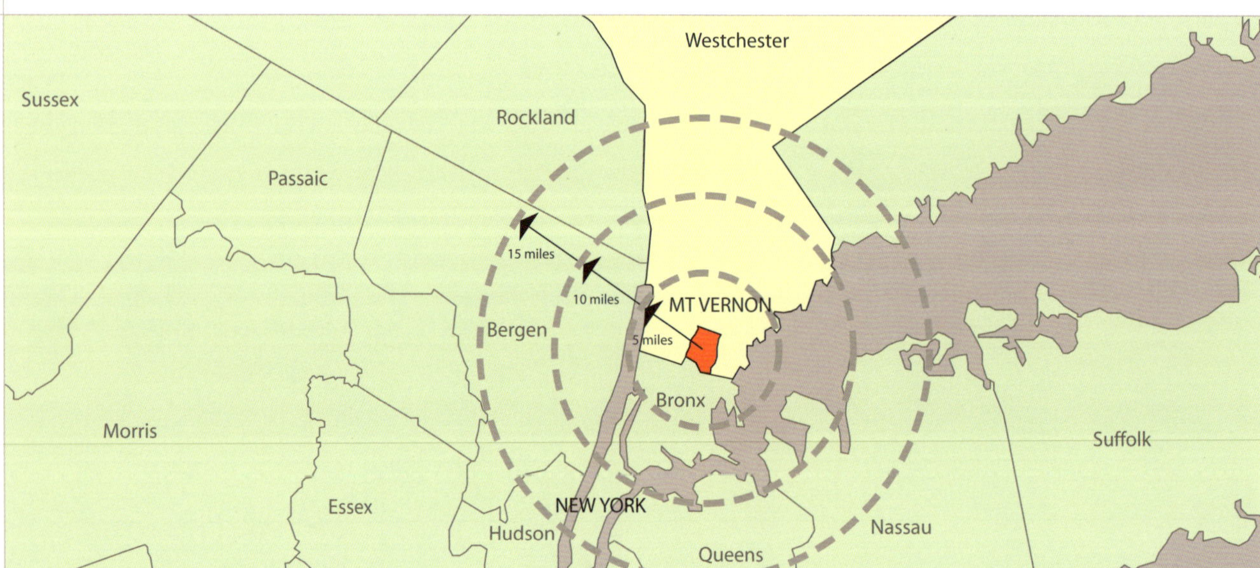

FACADE IMPROVEMENT

ELEMENTS OF A RENOVATED FACADE

Facade restorations

ARTS
DISTRICT

a

a. Existing storefront
b. Proposed arts venues

b

a

b

c

a. Fourth Avenue at Third Street
b. Proposed streetscape
c. Proposed streetscape

CALLE 106

CHAPTER 04

PARTNERS:

East 106th Street Steering Committee. Kenneth J. Knuckles, President and CEO, Upper Manhattan Empowerment Zone Development Corporation, Committee Chair.

CORPORATION

Upper Manhattan Empowerment Zone Development.

DATE OF PROJECT:

2004

Based on ideas put forward by community leaders, in 2004 the Upper Manhattan Empowerment Zone Development Corporation (UMEZ) initiated an exploration of design and development possibilities for East 106th Street, building on its unique physical assets and its status as a nexus of community and cultural life in East Harlem. UMEZ engaged the CCAC to help formulate a plan reflecting the community's vision. The subsequent study synthesizes concepts and recommendations that emerged from the CCAC's work with local stakeholders, covering 106th Street from Central Park to the East River—identified as the area's "cultural corridor"—and building off a core area at the "cultural crossroads" centered on the Lexington Avenue and 106th Street intersection and extending between Park and Third avenues.

The overall approach of the project included the following:

- Expressing the cultural identity of East 106th Street (and East Harlem) in the streetscape and outdoor spaces.
- Supporting small business development and storefront improvements, especially for existing businesses and those that contribute to the cultural corridor business cluster.
- Encouraging preservation of historic properties, including residential structures, while building local stakeholder equity.
- Creating partnerships for compatible infill development.

The CCAC compiled a report presenting ideas developed from an exploration of existing conditions, community perceptions, and previous studies. Stakeholder participation was gained through regular meetings

FARMACIA
Lex Drugs, Inc.
Tel. (212) 426-0402
Fax (212) 426-0403
CANDY
GROCERY
DELI OPEN
24 HRS.
ATM
CHINESE FOOD
ZAPATA
Newport
pleasure
to
Newport
SPECIAL OFFER
$ 6.00
Marlb

with a steering committee, convened by UMEZ to guide the study after the October 2004 Streetscape Design Workshop, and questionnaires circulated to community leaders and businesses. The report also reviewed earlier analyses and planning studies and included descriptions of district identity and community priorities underlying the design concepts and policy recommendations intended to express the cultural life of the community within the public space of the street. The goal of the project was to enliven the experience of the pedestrian, whether neighborhood resident or visitor.

The concept plan builds on these strategies and presents an inventory of major design proposals and recommendations. The plan balances the need for unifying streetscape elements that run the length of 106th Street within the area identified as the cultural corridor with the desire to implement unique measures at specific locations. The common features of lighting, street trees, and public art are intended to create coherence and a sense of unity within an identifiable district, while site-specific interventions are grouped into four distinct zones. The area around the Park Avenue Viaduct has been identified as a significant point of transition and separation.

The goals for the design concept and the CCAC's recommendations within each of these zones were as follows:

- **Zone 1**—Central Park/Museum Mile Connection
Improve the pedestrian link between Fifth and Park avenues, creating a sense of announcement and invitation into the cultural corridor.

- **Transition**—The Park Avenue Viaduct
Restore and improve the viaduct as a safe and visually appealing portal into the cultural crossroads.

- **Zone 2**—The Cultural Crossroads
Highlight and improve the cultural and historic assets between Park and Third avenues and on Lexington.

- **Zone 3**—Franklin Plaza Neighborhood
Strengthen the existing neighborhood-oriented business cluster in the blocks between Third and First avenues.

- **Zone 4**—East River Gateway
Capitalize on the East River Esplanade, the recreation pier at 107th Street, and Randall's Island, while announcing entry to the cultural corridor from the FDR Drive.

The CCAC's action plan for realizing this vision offered steps for implementing capital projects as well as policies or programs that support the broader goals. A map of public and private entities with jurisdiction over property along the corridor suggested some of the stakeholders who would need to be involved in spearheading change.

Although the overall vision for the area is quite comprehensive, the objective is not to overwhelm, but rather to view individual contributions and tangible improvements within a strategic framework that highlights opportunities for greater impact while expressing the community's vision.

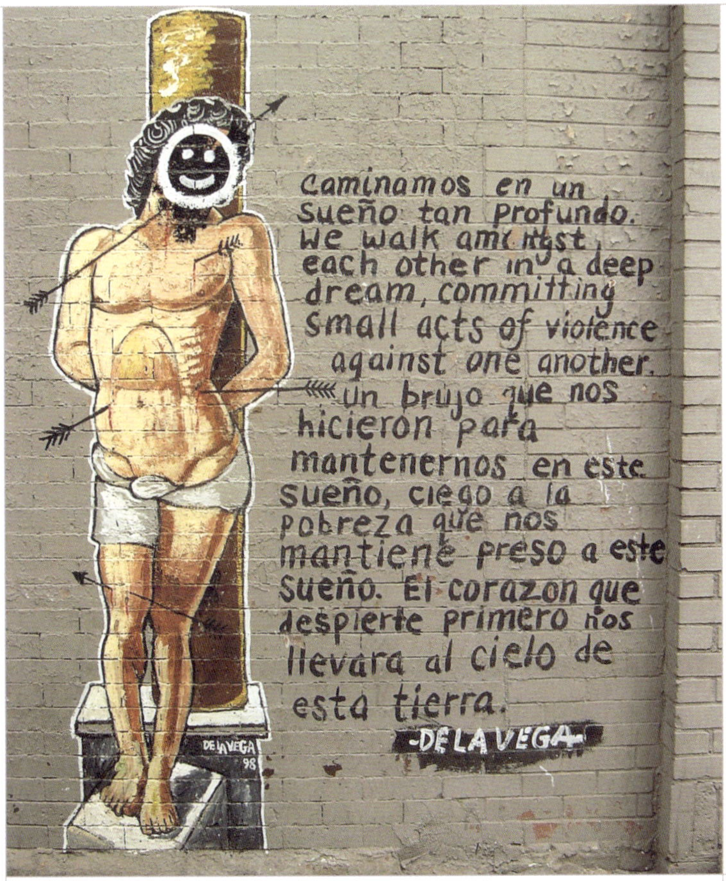

EXISTING CONDITIONS

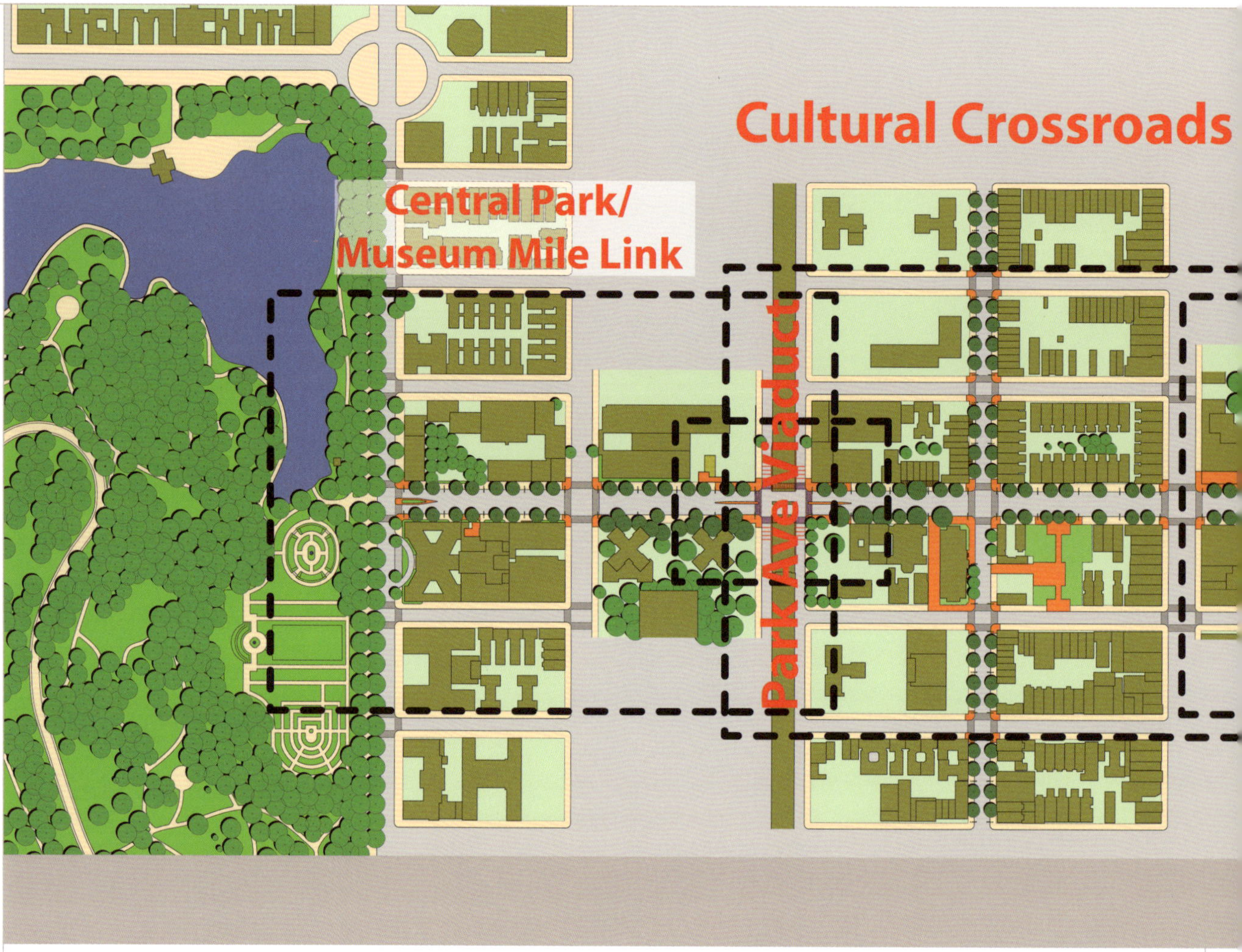

ZONE SPECIFIC
DESIGN CONCEPTS

In addition to the streetscape elements that apply throughout the Cultural Corridor, the plan outlines targeted design strategies for different stretches of this route. The study identifies four distinct "zones" heading from west to east, offering a unique set of solutions for each of these areas and the distinct assets and challenges they present. The Park Avenue Viaduct is a fifth point of focus, as it presents major difficulties and opportunities in transitioning between the first two zones. Design recommendations and targeted projects for each zone reflect strategies to enhance the diverse assets and functions within the corridor and crossroads as part of a unified whole.

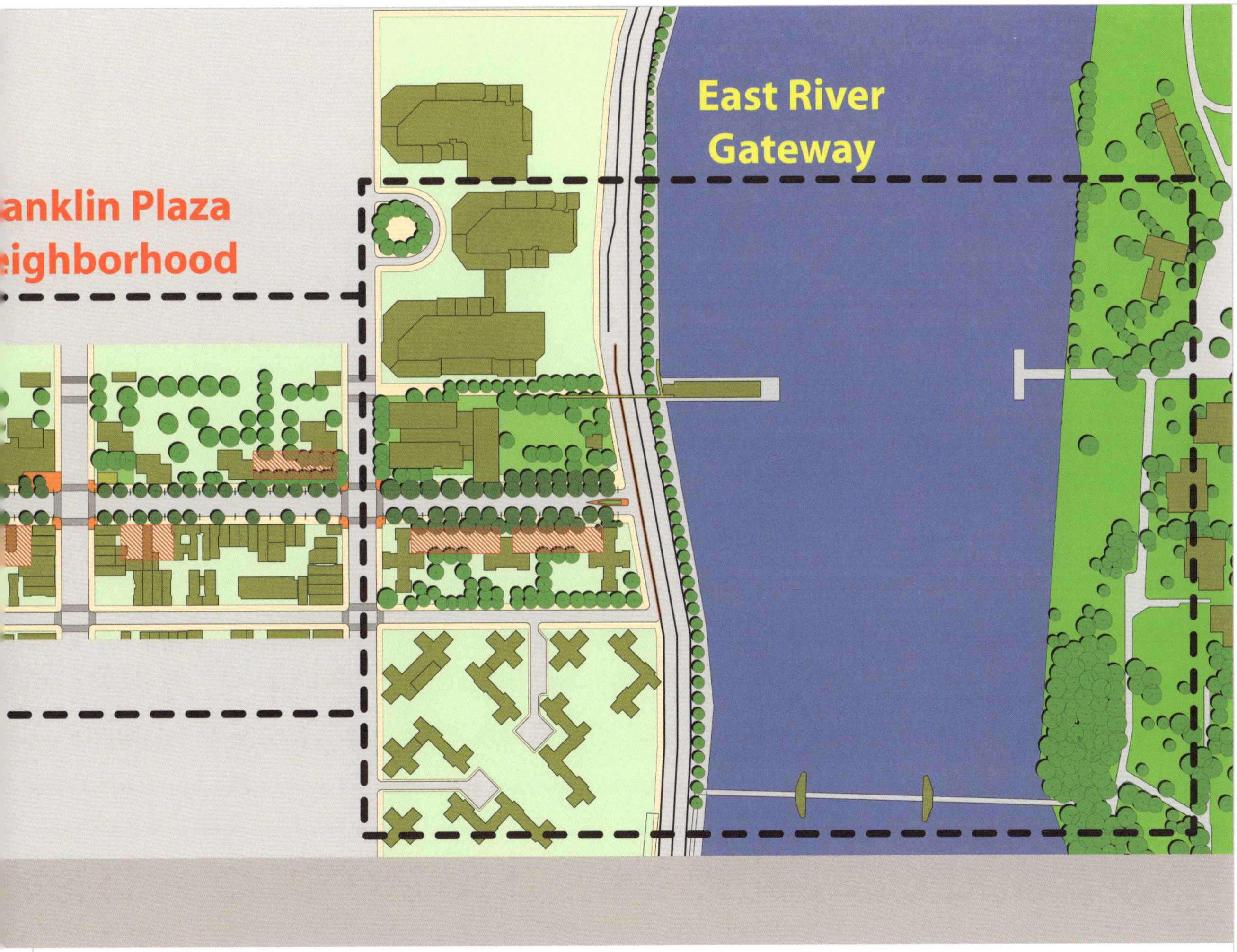
East River
Gateway
anklin Plaza
eighborhood

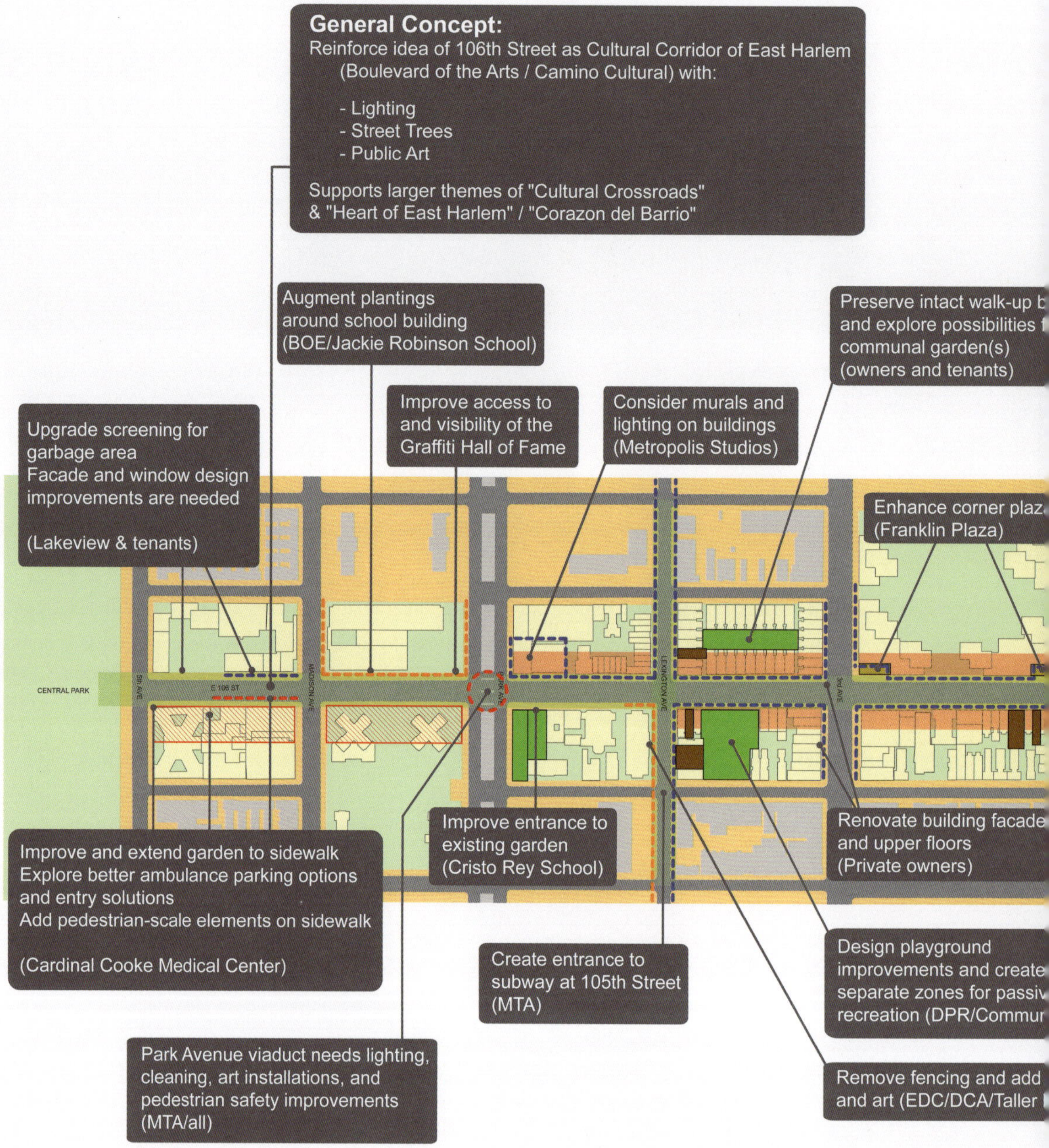
General Concept:
Reinforce idea of 106th Street as Cultural Corridor of East Harlem (Boulevard of the Arts / Camino Cultural) with:
- Lighting
- Street Trees
- Public Art
Supports larger themes of "Cultural Crossroads" & "Heart of East Harlem" / "Corazon del Barrio"
Augment plantings around school building (BOE/Jackie Robinson School)
Preserve intact walk-up and explore possibilities communal garden(s) (owners and tenants)
Improve access to and visibility of the Graffiti Hall of Fame
Consider murals and lighting on buildings (Metropolis Studios)
Upgrade screening for garbage area
Facade and window design improvements are needed
(Lakeview & tenants)
Enhance corner pla
(Franklin Plaza)
CENTRAL PARK
E 106 ST
Renovate building facad and upper floors (Private owners)
Improve entrance to existing garden (Cristo Rey School)
Improve and extend garden to sidewalk
Explore better ambulance parking options and entry solutions
Add pedestrian-scale elements on sidewalk
(Cardinal Cooke Medical Center)
Create entrance to subway at 105th Street (MTA)
Design playground improvements and create separate zones for passi recreation (DPR/Commu
Park Avenue viaduct needs lighting, cleaning, art installations, and pedestrian safety improvements (MTA/all)
Remove fencing and add and art (EDC/DCA/Taller

SITE ENHANCEMENTS
FACADE/STREETWALL ENHANCEMENTS
2ND AVENUE SUBWAY LINE
USABLE OPEN SPACE
POSSIBLE INFILL OPPORTUNITIES
COMMERCIAL OVERLAY
POSSIBLE INFILL FOR COMMUNITY OR CULTURAL USES
MAYOR PUBLIC IMPROVEMENTS NEEDED

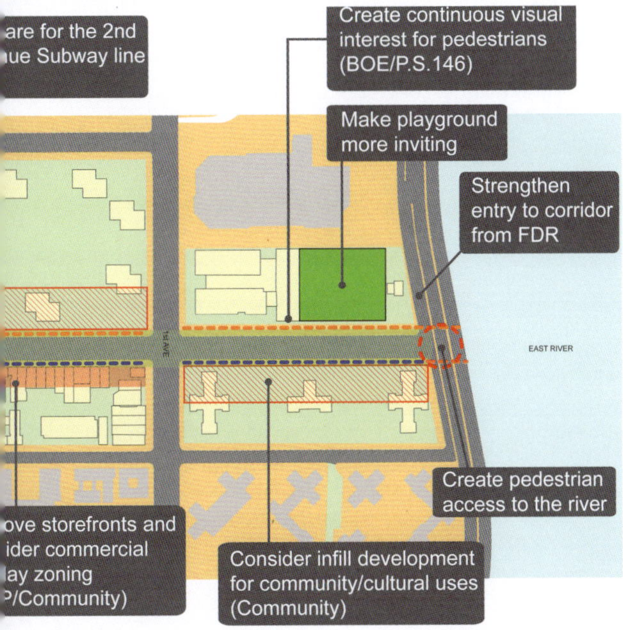

RECOMMENDATIONS
PUBLIC ART

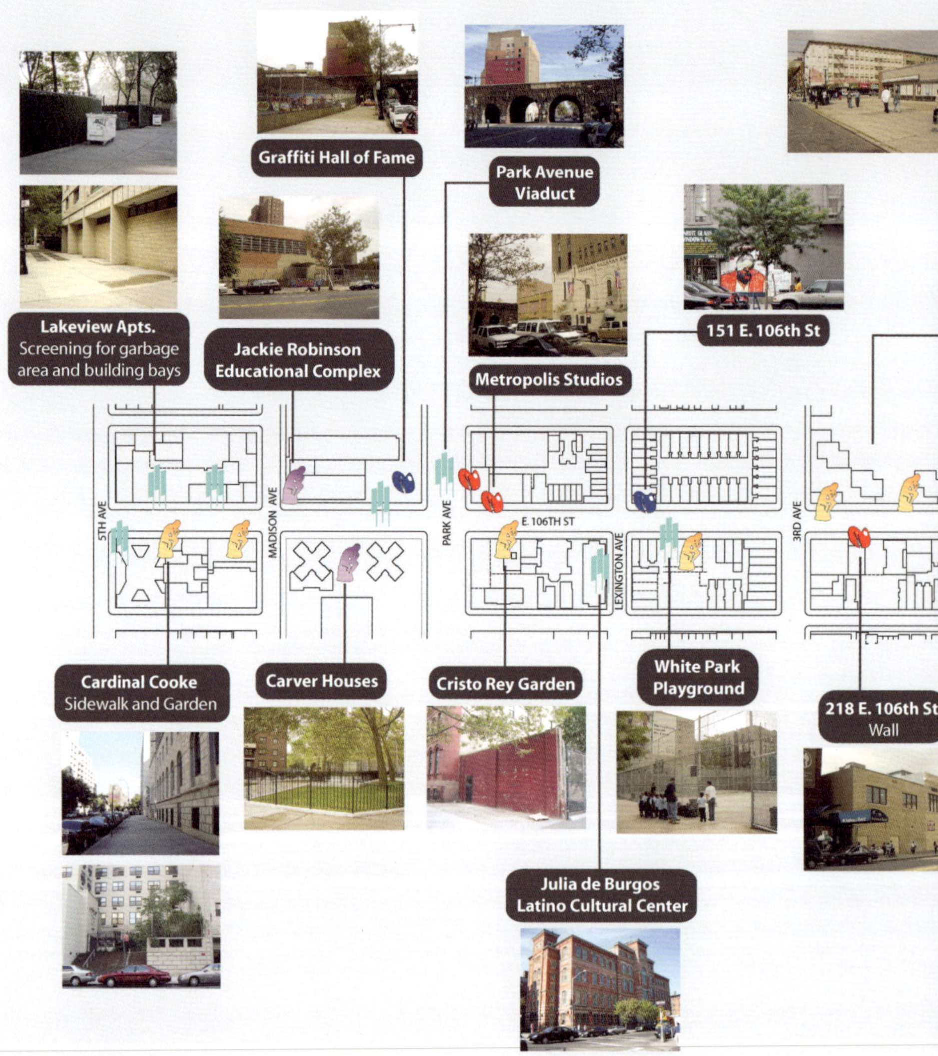

EXISTING SCULPTURE

PROPOSED SCULPTURE

OTHER PROPOSED ART INSTALLATIONS OR SIGNAGE

EXISTING MURAL

PROPOSED MURAL

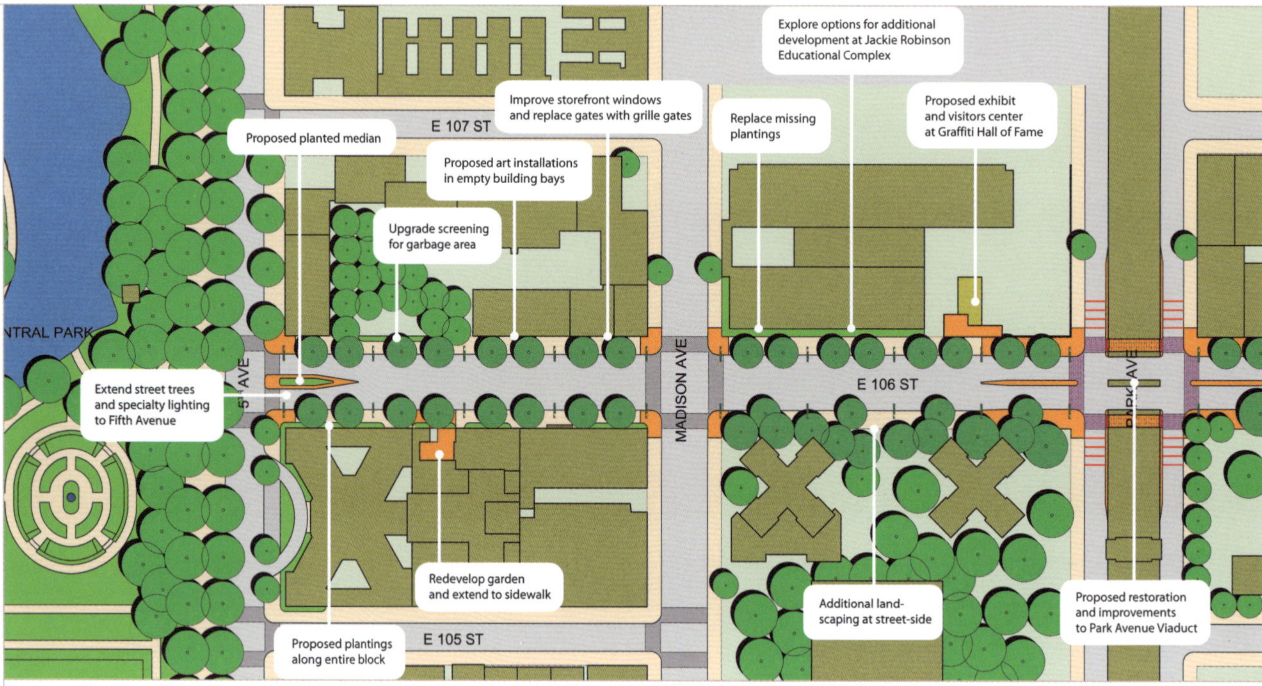

PROPOSED PLAN:

FIFTH AVENUE TO PARK AVENUE

PROPOSALS FOR ZONE 1

a. 106th street from Central Park
b. Park Avenue Viaduct gateway
c. Existing/Proposed terraced garden
d. Proposed screening for garbage area
e. Storefront improvement opportunity

a

METROPOLIS
LUMINOUS

b

c

d

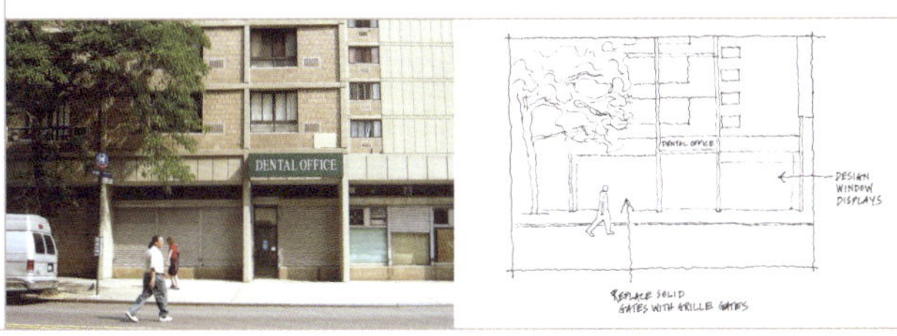
DENTAL OFFICE
DESIGN WINDOW DISPLAYS
REPLACE SOLID GATES WITH GRILLE GATES

e

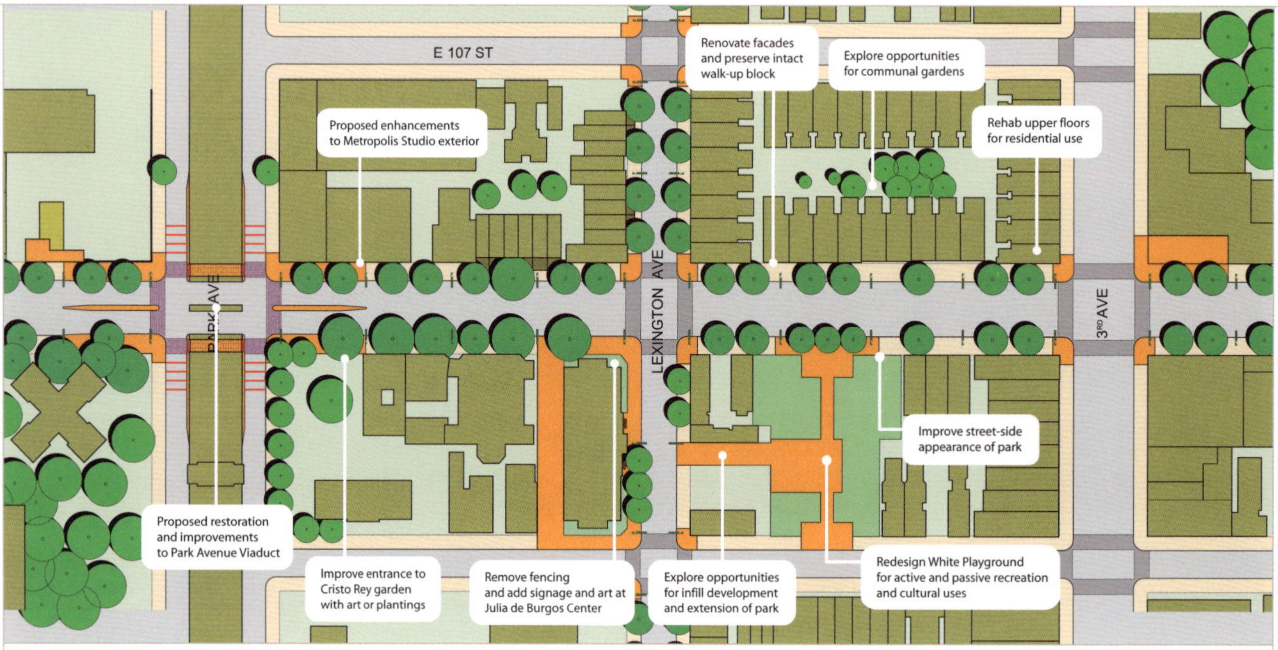

PROPOSED PLAN

PARK AVENUE TO THIRD AVENUE

ZONE 2
CULTURAL CROSSROADS

LEGEND

- EXISTING CULTURAL ANCHORS
- EXISTING CULTURE RELATED BUSINESSES
- PROPOSED CULTURE RELATED BUSINESSES
- EXISTING CHURCHES
- EXISTING SCHOOLS
- EXISTING ARTISTS HOUSING
- PROPOSED ARTISTS HOUSING
- OPEN SPACE

Strategy:

Highlight and improve the cultural and historic assets on 106th Street between Park and Third Avenues and on Lexington Avenue.

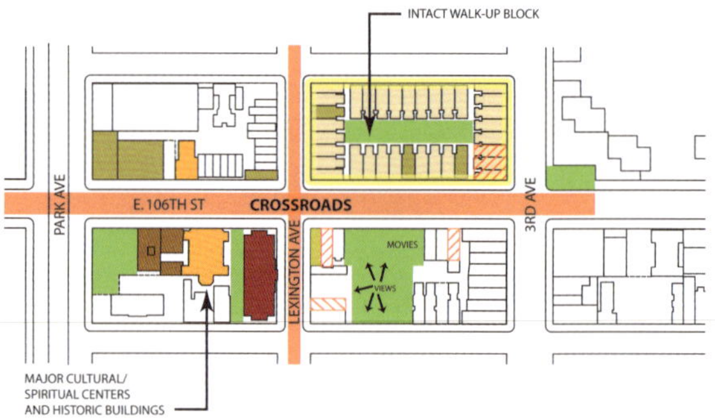

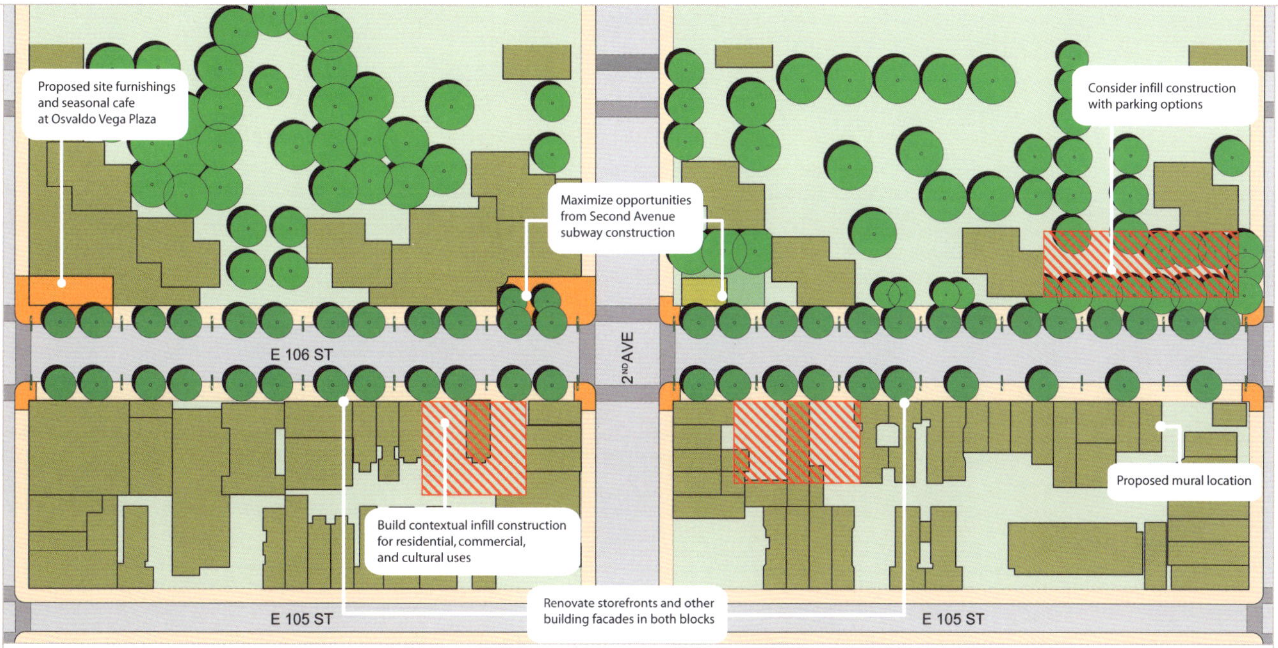

PROPOSED PLAN

THIRD AVENUE TO FIRST AVENUE

ZONE 3
FRANKLIN PLAZA NEIGHBOURHOOD

Strategy:

Strengthen the existing neighborhood-oriented business cluster in the blocks between First and Third Avenues.

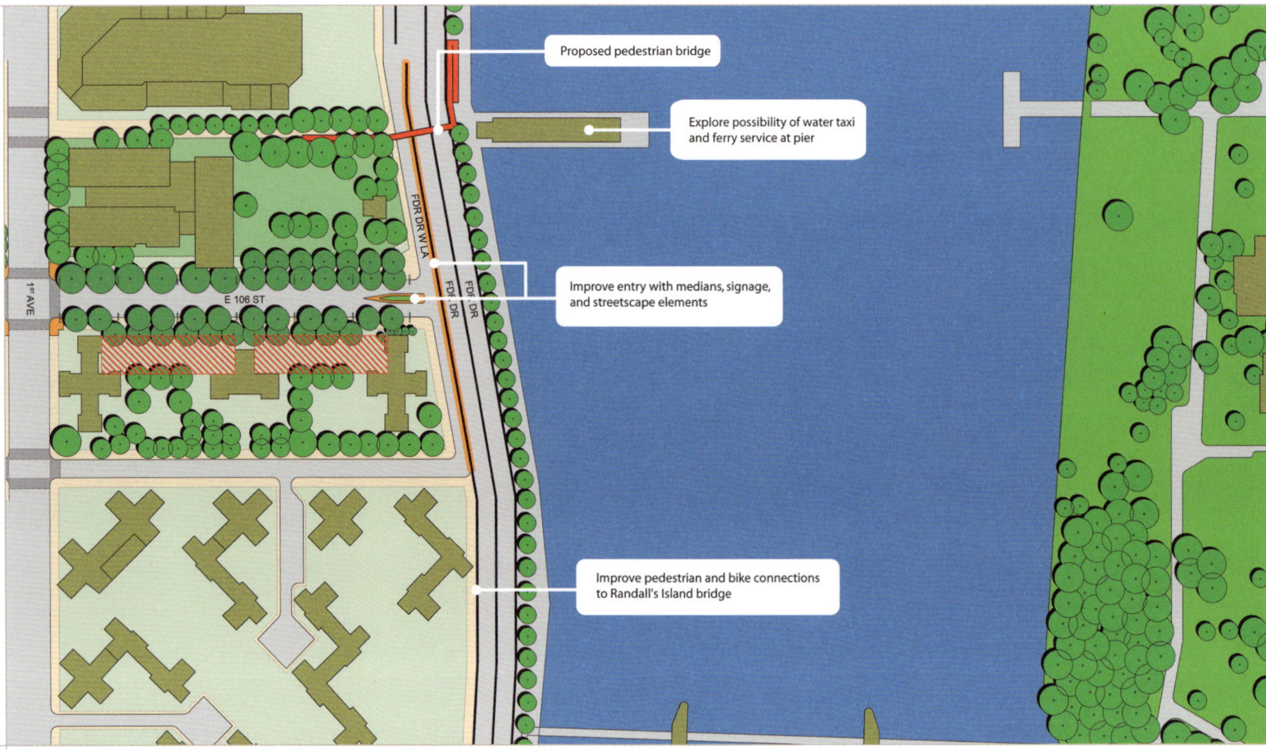

PROPOSED PLAN

FIRST AVENUE TO RANDALL'S ISLAND

ZONE 4
EAST RIVER GATEWAY

Strategy:

Capitalize on the East River Esplanade, the Recreation Pier at 107th Street and the proximity of Randall's Island, while announcing entry to the Cultural Corridor from the FDR Drive.

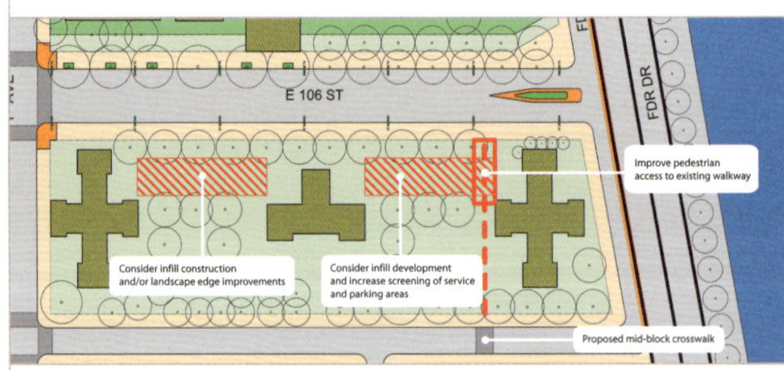

a

b

a. Proposed Plan. Wilson houses.
b. East River Gateway imagery.

BRADHURST NEIGHBORHOOD COMMERCIAL CORRIDOR & STREETSCAPE URBAN DESIGN STUDY

CHAPTER 04

PARTNERS:

Garrison McNeil Associated Architects & Alfred Eatman. Harlem Congregations for Community Improvement.

DATE OF PROJECT:

2008

Commissioned by Harlem Congregations for Community Improvement (HCCI) and conducted by the team of Alfred Eatman & Garrison McNeil Associates and the CCAC, the Bradhurst Urban Design Study focused on the commercial corridors in the Bradhurst neighborhood. The goal was to assess the general condition of the streetscape and commercial facades and identify potential for their improvement.

The Bradhurst neighborhood is located in Central Harlem in Upper Manhattan, in Community District 10. This forty-square block neighborhood between 155th and 138th streets is bounded on the west by Bradhurst Avenue and the natural border of Fordham Cliffs and on the east by Adam Clayton Powell Jr. Boulevard. Bradhurst is a self-contained neighborhood that still remains one of the poorest areas in New York City.

The Bradhurst neighborhood has been undergoing urban revitalization over the course of the last twenty years. The CCAC's urban design study contributed to this effort by looking at the Frederick Douglass Boulevard/Eighth Avenue commercial corridor between 144th and 155th streets. Research for the Bradhurst Commercial Corridor Study included several site visits, a neighborhood character analysis study, an inventory of all existing businesses, and detailed photographs for each block in the study area. This montage created a comprehensive description of the Bradhurst neighborhood. From this data and other existing information, the CCAC staff proceeded to generate design recommendations to improve both the legibility of the commercial corridors and to encourage the revitalization of underutilized vacant plots for the establishment of new businesses in the community.

The CCAC's recommendations called for creating a neighborhood "center of gravity" by concentrating commercial and retail establishments and providing for comfortable pedestrian movement through the area. This could be achieved by providing additional municipal parking to move cars off the street, as well as providing wider sidewalks with larger shade-giving trees, more street seating, better trash receptacles, and improved lighting coverage, both in the streets and under the aqueduct. A more inviting environment could be fostered by developing vacant lots as playgrounds or temporary community gardens and improving the traffic islands on Frederick Douglass Boulevard/Eighth Avenue. Establishing a year-round farmer's market would also improve the vitality of the neighborhood.

The CCAC report stressed that the most important factor in creating a successful business improvement district is encouraging the involvement of the local community board and civic groups, including Harlem Congregations for Community Improvement.

LAND USE MAP

RESIDENTIAL LAND USES

- ONE OR TWO FAMILY BUILDINGS
- MULTI-FAMILY BUILDINGS
- MIXED RESIDENTIAL AND COMMERCIAL BUILDINGS

NON-RESIDENTIAL LAND USES

- COMMERCIAL / OFFICE BUILDINGS
- INDUSTRIAL / MANUFACTURING
- OPEN SPACE AND OUTDOOR RECREATION
- PUBLIC FACILITIES AND INSTITUTIONS
- TRANSPORTATION AND UTILITY
- PARKING FACILITIES
- VACANT LAND
- ALL OTHERS OR NO DATA

NEIGHBORHOOD MAP

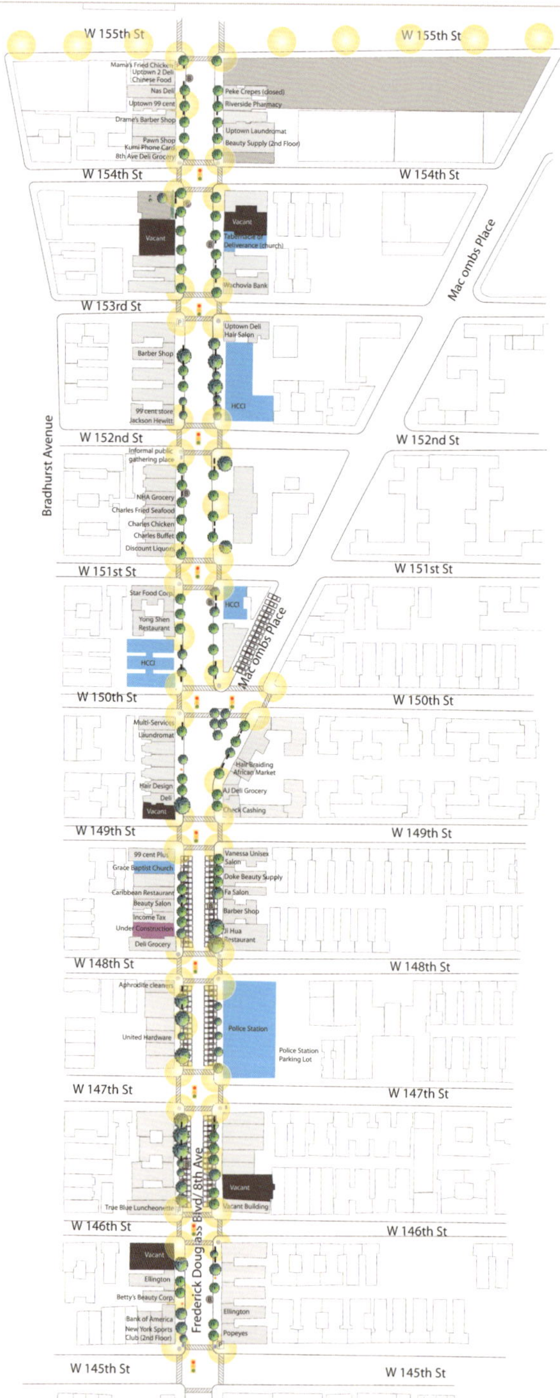

a

PROPOSED STREETSCAPE

a. Bikelanes
b. Harlem gateway post
c. 145th street gateway
d. Bradhurst commercial district
e. Viaduct

b

Proposed

Existing conditions

c

d

Existing conditions

Proposed

e

GUN HILL ROAD / WEBSTER AVENUE STUDY

CHAPTER 04

PARTNERS:

Mosholu Preservation Corporation.
Montefiore Medical Center.

DATE OF PROJECT:

2003

The CCAC partnered with the Mosholu Preservation Corporation and a community support corporation sponsored by Montefiore Medical Center to study the development potential of a site at Gun Hill Road and Webster Avenue in the northwest Bronx. The site sits at a major crossroads between two stable working-class communities adjacent to an on-ramp for the Bronx River Parkway and the planned Bronx River Greenway, straddling a Metro-North Raiload station.

Through research, analysis, and discussions with stakeholders such as the Metropolitan Transportation Authority/Metro-North, the CCAC's student interns explored alternative scenarios for the site incorporating residential, commercial, and recreational uses that exploit the unique assets of the site and address the challenges for its development.

The CCAC summarized its findings in a report aiming to spur discussion among city administrators, the community, and local institutions about this site and its surroundings within a new land-use framework.

Track 3

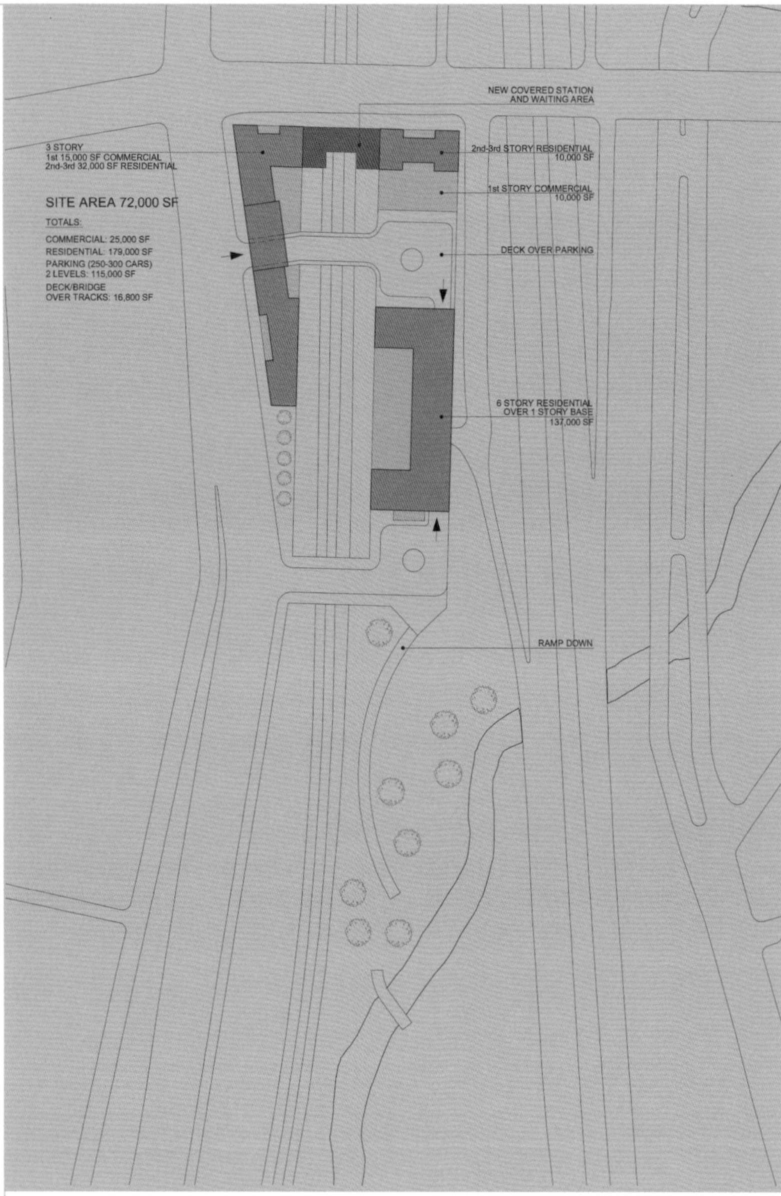

R7-1 MIXED RESIDENTIAL & COMMERCIAL

GUN HILL RD / WEBSTER AVE. STUDY - BRONX, NY

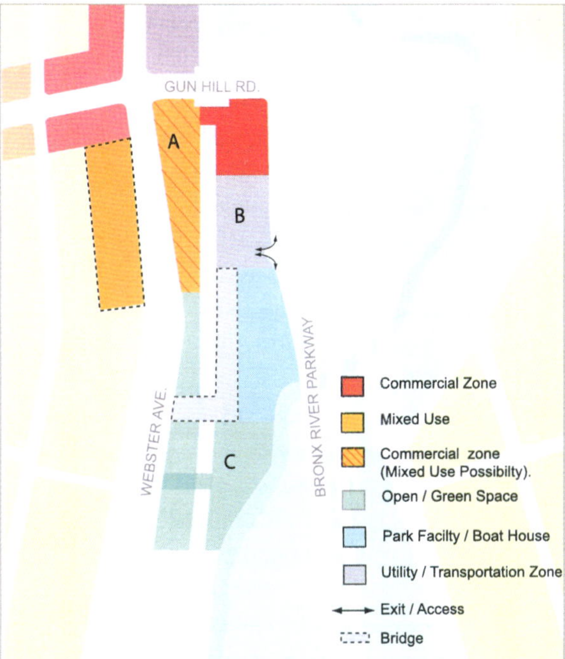

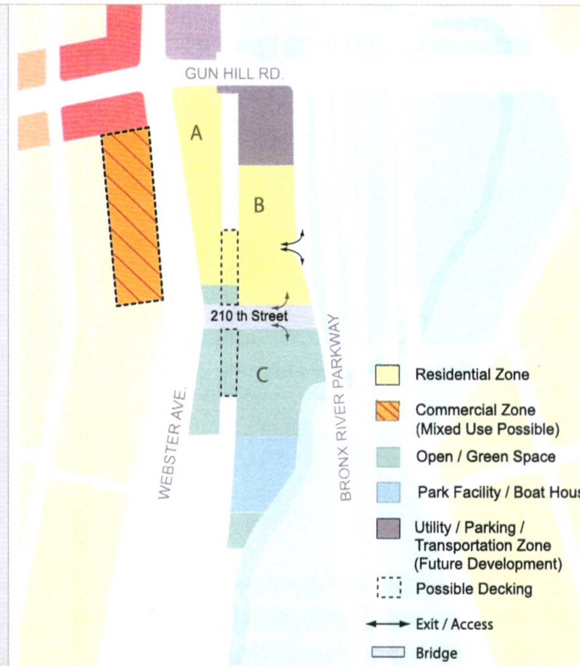

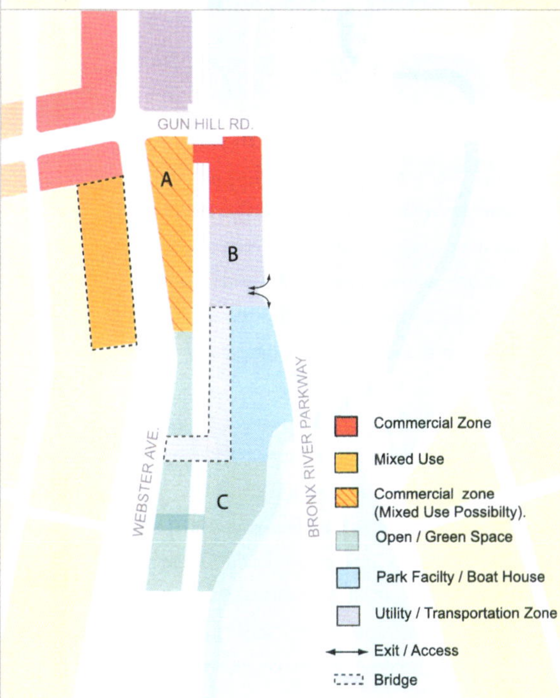

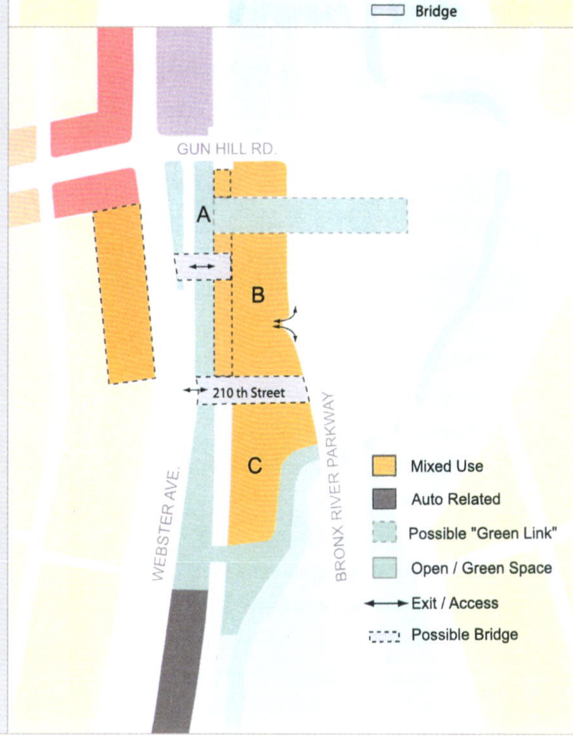

GUN HILL ROAD PROPOSALS

Previous page. Gun Hill Road drawing.

Previous page. Gun Hill Road model
This page. Gun Hill Road model

CHAPTER 05

PROJECT DESIGN

LIBRARY LANE

CHAPTER 05

PARTNERS:

Fordham Bedford Housing Corporation. Sistas and Brothas United, Northwest Bronx Community and Clergy Coalition.

DATE OF PROJECT:

2001 - present

In 2001, the CCAC was asked by the Fordham Bedford Housing Corporation, a community housing advocacy organization in the Kingsbridge neighborhood in the Bronx, to look into the restoration of Coles Lane. The site runs east from the front of the new Bronx Library Center, facing a trash-strewn alley and fronting on the historic Edgar Allan Poe Cottage.

The Fordham Bedford Housing Corporation saw the project, dubbed "Library Lane," as an opportunity to unite the area as a cultural site, providing gardens and public open space. The CCAC saw an additional opportunity for a demonstration project highlighting the reuse of materials, the power of public/private partnership, and the application of sustainability and accessibility principles.

Library gatherings of young people, local business owners, and public meetings of the local community board all offered a chance for discussion between stakeholders and designers and community input to the concept plan.

The resulting design is currently in phase one of construction. The project has sparked a relationship between the CCAC and Sistas and Brothas United, part of the Northwest Bronx Community and Clergy Coalition. Committed to improving education and empowering youth in their community, the group has launched a proposal to create a community center in the currently vacant old library building.

EMPEÑO
24 HOURS
LAST STOP REALTY
Sales
Rentals
Residential
Commercial
LAST STOP REALTY
367-3233
STOP

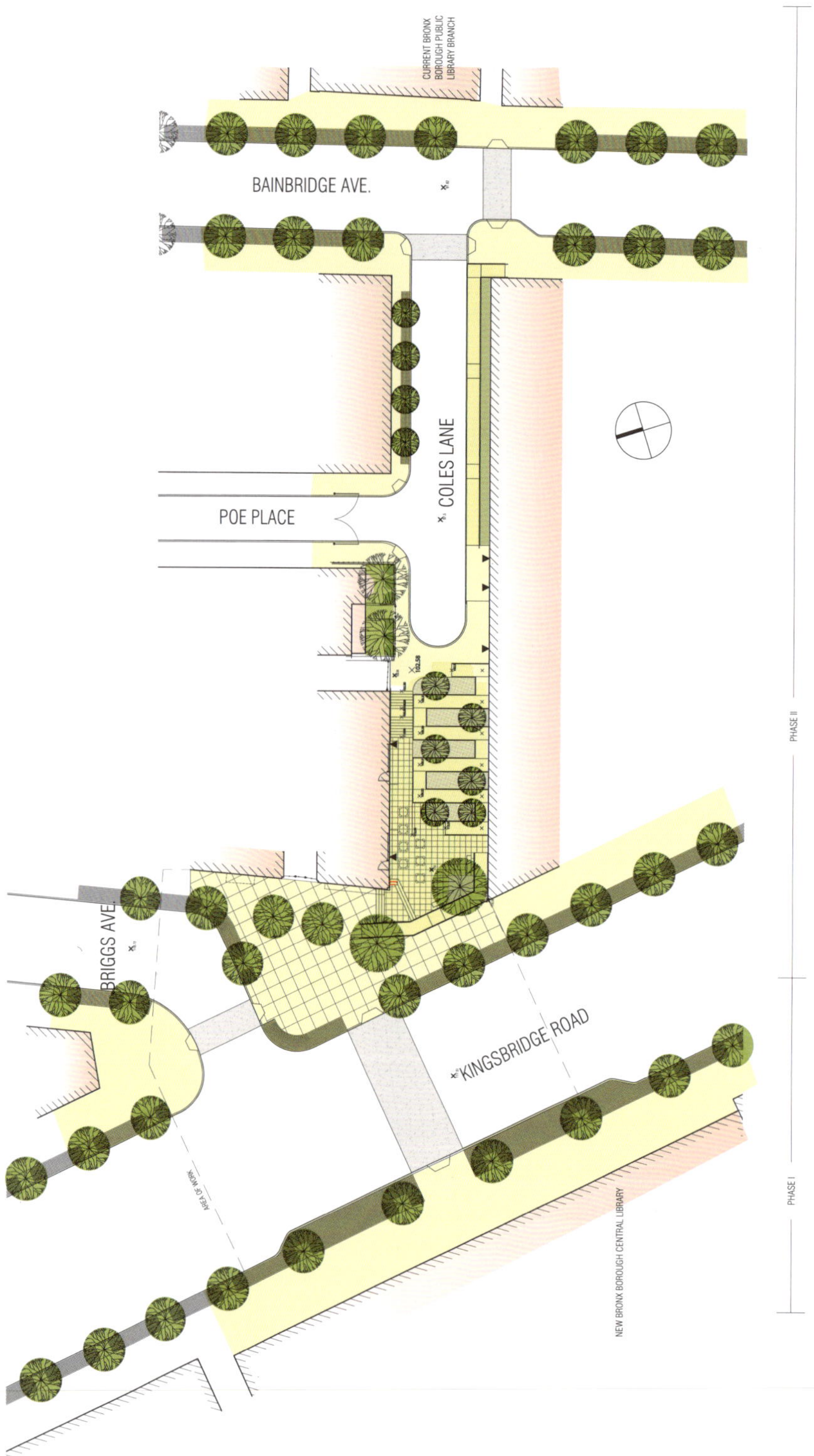
CURRENT BRONX BOROUGH PUBLIC LIBRARY BRANCH
BAINBRIDGE AVE.
COLES LANE
POE PLACE
PHASE II
BRIGGS AVE.
KINGSBRIDGE ROAD
PHASE I
NEW BRONX BOROUGH CENTRAL LIBRARY

a

b

c

d

a. Master Plan
b. Location map
c. Library Lane model
d. Existing conditions
e. Community charrette

e

After

BEFORE / AFTER STUDIES

Before

After

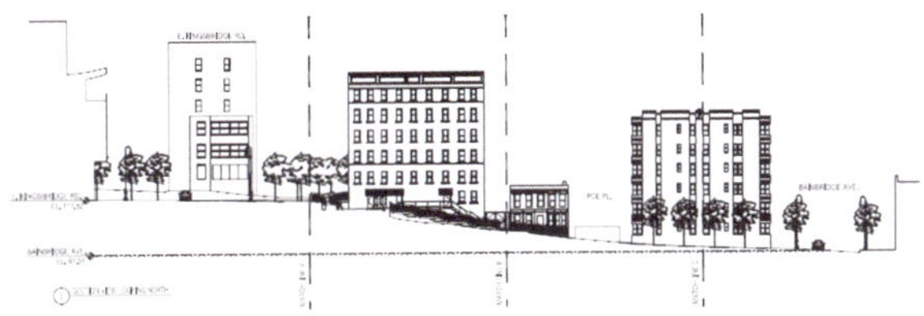

Before

After

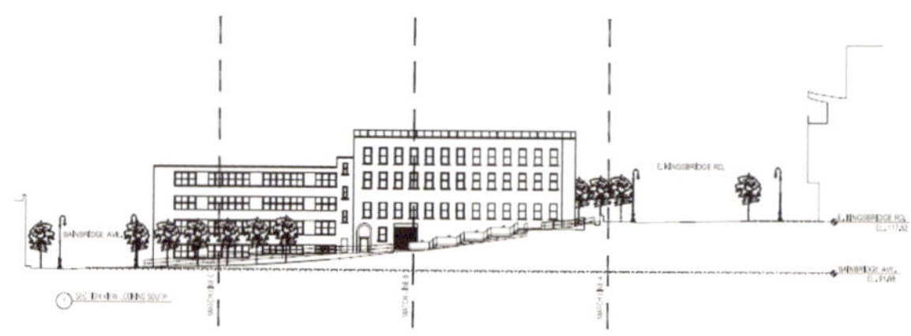

Before

After

BEFORE / AFTER STUDIES

Before

MOSHOLU MONTEFIORE COMMUNITY CENTER

CHAPTER 05

PARTNERS:

Lehman College Department of Nursing.
Mark Kates/Dorothy Schuster Architects.
HUD Hispanic-Serving Institutions Assisting Communities Grant.

DATE OF PROJECT:

2004 - 2005

With the support of a Hispanic-Serving Institutions Assisting Communities Grant from the U.S. Department of Housing and Urban Development, the CCAC designed and submitted working documents for this 2,500-square-foot renovation of community center facilities in the northwest Bronx. CCAC student interns worked in association with the Lehman College Department of Nursing and Mark Kates/Dorothy Schuster Architects.

The project entailed reconfiguring former storage and mechanical rooms to house program space for youth training, visual arts and media classrooms, as well as a copy shop and a superintendent's office. Construction began in the summer of 2006.

MOSHOLU MONTEFIORE COMMUNITY CENTER

FLOOR PLAN

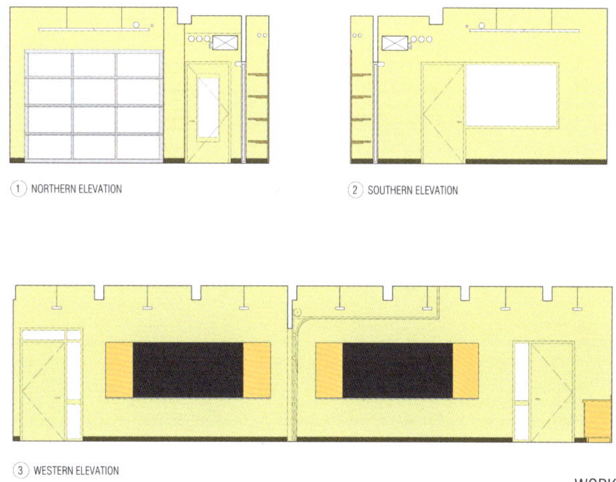

WORKSHOP W

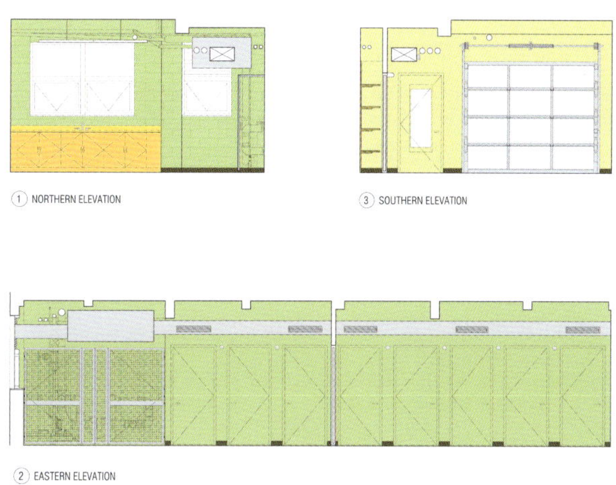

WORKSHOP E

LIZA TORRES-SAEZ CHILDREN´S PARK

CHAPTER 05

PARTNERS:

Fordham Bedford Housing Corporation.

DATE OF PROJECT:

2005 - 2006

Fordham Bedford Housing Corporation (FBHC) in the northwest Bronx provides affordable housing for residents, managing nearly thirty thousand apartments. Originally named Briggs Mini Park, the site is a small recreational area situated between two FBHC apartment buildings, intended to serve the children who reside there. The lot was heavily used, yet maintenance was neglected. The site became strewn with garbage; the equipment was rusted and dangerous; the surrounding twenty-foot high chain-link fence had deteriorated and the twelve-foot retaining wall was crumbling. In addition, the lot could be accessed only down a precipitous slope. At the time the CCAC became involved, Briggs Mini Park faced condemnation for safety and accessibility reasons.

At the request of the FBHC, the CCAC created a new design for the lot and helped to supervise its construction. The design included a play structure designed to code, an ADA-compliant sitting area and ramp leading to a set of steps for access into the park, and new plantings. The repair of the retaining wall and new fences enhanced the appearance of the lot and were well received by the abutting residents. The renamed Liza Torres-Saez Children's Park officially opened with more than two hundred residents in attendance at the dedication ceremony. In July 2008 an ongoing summer youth program was initiated at the park.

LIZA TORRES-SAEZ
CHILDREN'S
PARK
Dedicated July 31, 2008

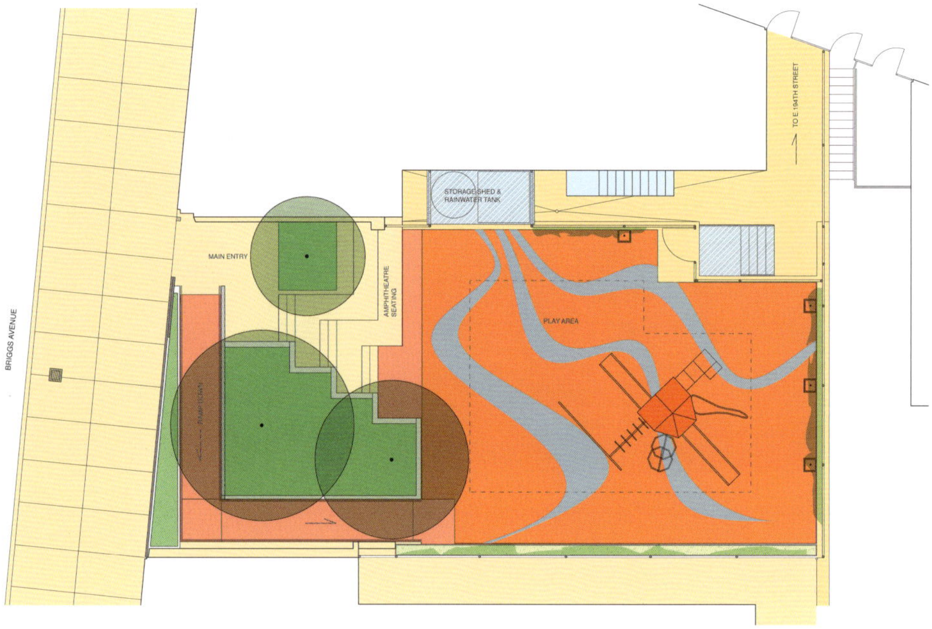

a

a. Proposed Plan
b. Entry ramp
c. Playground
d. Existing conditions
e. Existing conditions

b

c

d

e

a

a. Previous conditions
b. Sketch
c. Existing conditions

b

c

HEALTH CENTER PLAZA

CHAPTER 05

PARTNERS:

Heritage Health and Housing.

DATE OF PROJECT:

2009

The need for improvements to the plaza on the corner of Amsterdam Avenue and 146th Street, which is surrounded by city-owned facilities, prompted Heritage Health and Housing to request planning help from the CCAC. The CCAC prepared drawings for the demolition of the existing signage and air intakes in the plaza and developed design sketches for repaving and planting, as well as a design for an obelisk/information sign. The adjacent building houses a preschool for developmentally disabled toddlers and needed a protected and enclosed play area, which was designed for them by the CCAC.

Remember
Me

a

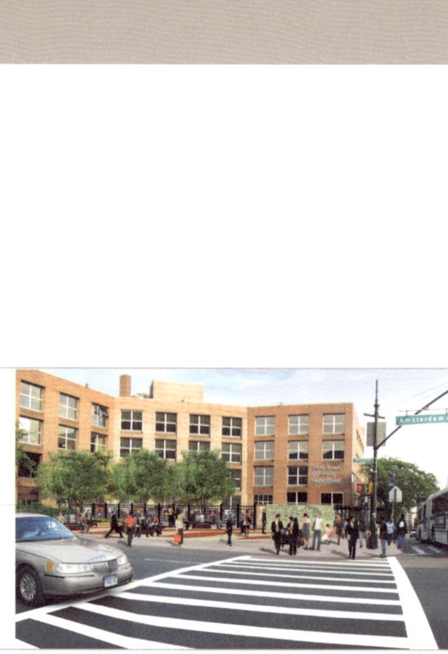

b

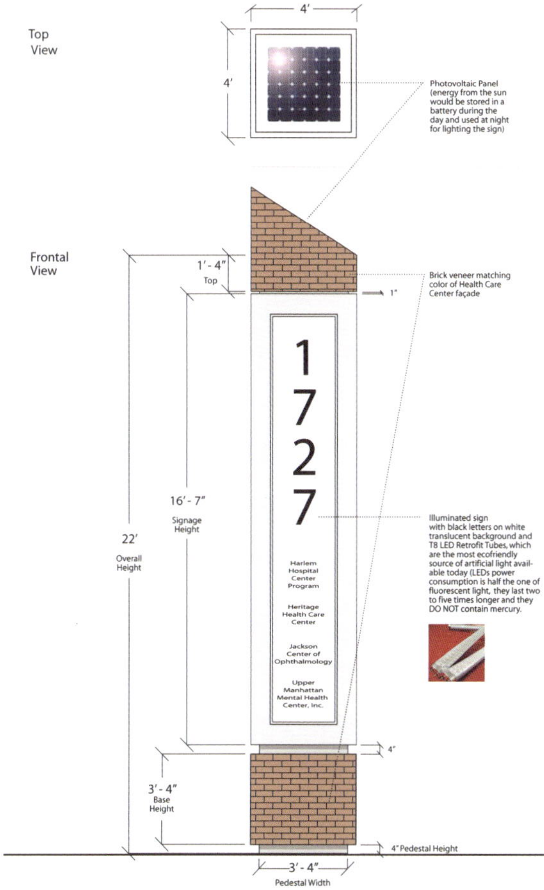

c

a. Before/After
b. Rendering
c. Proposed obelisk
d. Sketch

d

PROJECT CREDITS

PAST GRANTS AWARDED TO CCAC

Rockefeller Brothers Fund Grant
City of New York Department of Cultural Affairs
The City College of New York
Surdna Foundation Grant
JP Morgan Chase
Housing Preservation Development (HPD)
Housing and Urban Development (HUD)
Harlem Urban Development Corporation
George Willett
National Endowment for the Arts (NEA)

COMMUNITY PARTNERS

Councilman Robert Jackson, NYC Council

Amalgamated Housing Cooperative
Doris Spencer, Director of Education

New York Charter School Association
Lorraine Barcant

Bronx Jewish Community Council
Brad Silver, Director

Bronx Community Board 5
Dana Driscoll, Department of City Planning

CB5 BCC Campus, McCracken Hall
Xavier Rodriguez

Central Park Scholars
Central Park Conservancy
Curtis Dann – Messier, Education Programs Coordinator
John Riddick
Greta Schiller, 9th Grade Lead Educator, Central Park Scholars
JoAnn Schneider, Education Programs Coordinator,
Central Park Conservancy

Rachel Stephenson, Director of Education,
Central Park Conservancy

East Harlem Preservation
Marina Ortiz
Debbie Quinones
Fernando Salicruz
Niki

Fordham Bedford Housing Cooperation
Patrick Logan, Director of Development, FBHC
Rosanna Viera, Development Coordinator, FBHC

Harlem Community Development Corporation
Wayne Benjamin, Architect, Chair – Land Use Committee
Thomas G. Lunke, Director of Planning
Francisco Guzman, Architect

Community District 12
Community Board 12 Manhattan
Aaron Scott
Ebenezer Smith, District Manager of CB12
Debra Blow, Finance Director District 12M
Charles DeFino, Manager District 12M

The Neighborhood Planning and Land Use Study Funding:
Lilliam Perez – New York State Senator Eric Sneiderman
Anthony Borelli, Manhattan Office of the Borough President, Scott Stringer
Working Group:
Martin Collins, Board Chair 2004-6
Anita Barberis, Assistant Chair
Samelys Lopez, Urban Planning Fellow
James Berlin, Board Member – Traffic and Transportation
Sybil Dodson Lucas, Chair – Aging
Julissa Gomez, Board Member – Public Safety
Julio Rodriguez, Board Member (no longer)
Dora Maria Abreu, Board Member – Land Use
Ruddy Santana, Board Member – Economic Development
Vivian Ducat, Board Member Land Use
Steve Simon, Chair – Health and Environment
Manny Velazquez – Board Chair 2007
Jeffrey Laufer
Atlantic Chapter – Sierra Club

Board Staff Support
Hugh Mitchell, John Culpepper, Conservation Chairperson,

Erasing Boundaries – Pennsylvania/New York Campus Compact Consortium
Kate Dantsin, Project Manager, Learn & Serve Grant
New York Campus Compact
James Heffernan, Executive Director
Pennsylvania Campus Compact
Dr. Charlene Gray, Executive Director
Center for Community Design Research
SUNY – Environmental Science & Forestry
Maren King

Center for Community Planning and Development
Hunter College/CUNY
Rebecca Ferguson, Research Assistant

Research Foundation of CUNY
Marek Sujol, Project Administrator

OPRD of Syracuse University
Ellen Rougeux Evaluator

Office of Professional Research & Development,
Syracuse University Continuing Education
Hayley Cavino, Evaluation Coordinator
The Research Foundation of The City University of New York
Richard F. Rothbard, President
Planning Division
Denise Edens

New York City Department of Transportation
Theodore Oberman, Executive Director Capital Project & Initiation

Office of the Bronx Borough Commissioner

Rockaway / Greenway
Greater Woodhaven Development Corporation
Stephen Esposito – President
Maria A. Thomson – Executive Director
National Park Service, Rivers & Trails Program
Joanne Dittersdorf

New York City Council
Dennis Gallagher

TVG Studio NYC
Forest Hills Little League, Inc.
Joseph R. Nocerino – Vice Chairman

RGGB
Jordan Sandke

Village of Hempstead Development Agency
Mayor Wayne J. Hall – Chairman
Dr. Ivory Holmes – Vice Chair
Mr. Inocenio Perdomo – Secretary

Hempstead Village – The Hub
Village of Hempstead
Claude Gooding, Commissioner – Community Development
James York, Representative
Jewel Butler, Representative

Incorporated Village of Hempstead
Community Development Agency
Latasha Conyers

Hempstead High school
Gregory J. de Bruin, PE, PLS, Partner
De Bruin Civil Engineers & Land Surveyors
A. James de Bruin & Sons, LLP
Chai Davidson, Assistant Principal
New York State DOT
Mr. McCulloch, Engineer

New York State Department Division of Coastal Resources
Jaime Reppert, Coordinator

Heritage Health and Housing
Mr. Jorge L. Abreu, LCSW, Executive Director Heritage Health Housing Corp.

Dr. John Jay Cardwell, Board Chairman
LaQuita Henry, Project Manager

City College of New York
Gregory Williams, President
Lois Cronholm, Chief of Operations

NYS Division of Housing and Community Renewal
NYS Housing Trust Fund Corporation
Judith A. Calogero, Commissioner and Chairperson

The Office of Community Development
New York Main Street Program
Sidney Parker

Friends of Montefiore Park
Ms. Alida De Palma, Founder
Joe Henriquez McNearney

The City College Libraries
Hope Community, Inc.
HUD Office of University Partnerships
Temple Emanuel at Parkchester
P.S. 192 Jacob Schiff School
Design Corps/CCAC
Upper Manhattan Empowerment Zone
Montefiore School Health Program
Enterprise Foundation
Community Board 9 – Manhattan
Community Board 3 – Manhattan / Waterfront Task Force
Legal Aid Society of Rockland County
Cathedral Baptist Church
Mosholu Montefiore Community Center
Mosholu Preservation Corporation (MPC)
Lower Manhattan Cultural Council
Baruch College Newman Real Estate Institute
South Bronx Overall Economic Development Corp. (SOBRO)
Life Changers Church
ACAB Corporation
Harlem Valley Heights CDC
Astella Community Development Corp.
The Cherry Tree Assoc. Inc.
West Harlem Art Fund
Habitat for Humanity NY
Reservoir Keeper's House
Community League of the Heights
Municipal Art Society / Imagine NY
Office of the Bronx Borough President
Audubon Partnership for Economic Development

Crosstown 116, Lance Jay Brown and Robert L Geddes

Northern Manhattan Heritage Project, Lance Jay Brown
and Ethel Sheffer

Ibo Balton, Director of Project Planning, NYC Department of
Housing Preservation and Development (HPD)
Larry Racioppo, photographer

The Museum of the City of New York Research Department
Abyssinian Development Corporation
Harlem Congregations for Community Improvement
GRID Properties
Full Spectrum
The Museum for African Art
Richard Dattner Architects
Aero-industrial Communications
Skidmore Owings and Merrill
W-architecture and Landscape Architecture
Rogers Marvel Architecture
Ten Arquitectos
Harlem Children's Zone
NYC Department of Parks and Recreation

DEANS
DIRECTORS

DEANS, ACTING DEANS, AND CHAIRS

Bernard P. Spring
Founding Dean
1968 – 1980

Rosaria Piomelli
Dean
1980 – 1983

Donals Mintz
Acting Dean
1983 – 1985

J. Max Bond Jr.
Dean
1985 – 1991

Gordon A. Gebert
Acting Dean
1991 – 1995

Donald Ryder
Chair
1995 – 1998

Lance Jay Brown
Chair and Director, 1998 – 2001 and Chair, 2001– 2004

George Ranalli
Dean
1999 – present

LIST OF DIRECTORS AND ASSOCIATE AND ASSISTANT DIRECTORS OF CCAC

Luis Aponte Pares
Director
1980 – 1984

Kevin Johnson
Assistant Director
1980 – 1984

Lance Jay Brown
Director
1985 – 1988

Jonathan Ochshorn
Associate Director

Stephen A. Cambell
Associate Director
1987 – 1988

Ghislaine Hermanuz
Director
1988 – 1998

Anthony Cruson
Associate Director
1988 – 1990

D.C. Dunham
Assistant Director
1988

Michael Koehler
Associate Director
1991

Ethan Cohen
Director
1999 – 2006

Marilyn Gallagher
Associate Director
1993 – 2001

Denisha Williams
Project Associate
2002 – 2005

Achva Benzinberg Stein
Director
2007 – present

Holly Kallman
Assistant Director
2007 – 2009

CCAC STAFF

Gallagher, Marilyn
Associate Director

Gonzalez, Juan
Project Coordinator – Survey
Graphics

Regul, Julia
Project Manager

Kallman, Holly
Assistant Director
Project Manager

Karantzalis, Maria
Studio Manager / Team Leader

Leyton, Rodolfo
Project Director – Graphics

Li, Timothy
Zoning 3D Graphics

Prieto, Johanna
Survey Development
GIS

Urcia, Eduard
Project Coordinator – Survey
Graphics

Williams, Denisha
Assistant Director
Project Manager

Cross, Charles
GIS, Landscape Architecture

CONSULTANTS SELECTED

Angotti, Thomas
Professor of Urban Planning and Director
Center for Community Planning and Development
Hunter College / CUNY

Bagchee, Nandine
Architect, Consultant

Curry, Rex L.
Reid Curry Inc. – Strategic Planning
Brooklyn, NY

FxFowle Architects, PC
John J. Loughran, AIA, PP, AICP, LEED™
Associate

Giordano, Trudy
Graphic Artist
Brooklyn, New York

Hansen, Laura
Program Officer
The J.M. Kaplan Fund

Stein, J. David
Urban and Regional Planning – Transportation Planning
Jersey City, NJ

Urbitran
Vice President
Atma R. Sookram, AICP, PP, MT

Lee Weintraub
Landscape Architecture
Yonkers NY

Younge, Lesley
9th Grade Asst. Educator,
Central Park Scholars

STUDENTS

Laura Hansen (project coordinator)
Ghiora Aharoni
Peter Brassard
Gregory Salandy
Rony Dawood
Silvia Jenatschke
Maria Karantzalis
Burak Kasapoglu
Jeffry Keiter
Robert M. Rodriguez
Eduard Urcia
Marco Williamson
Charles Cross
Rafael Jaquez
Laila Al Khayer
Nigel Ann LaQua
Francisco Lopez
Rafael Olivo
Denisha Williams
Owen Detlor
Lior Schapiro
John Alvarado
Brenda Bello
David de Jesus
Reinaldo Garcia
Kerstin Gust
Davis Iszard
Daniel Isoldi
Marcel Jaloveckas
Danny Wai Lam
Sangzo Lee
Vladimir Rigueur
Joel Rivera
Costas Tsangarides
Ronen Wilk
Antje Zabka
Christopher Zerbo
Meital Ben-Shimon
Chaio-Heng Chen
Hyun-Soo Kim
Nadia Nilina
Juan Gonzalez
Timothy Li
Patty Jatkowski

Ana Travarez
John Vlahakis
Pablo Patino
Wennian Qu
Jenny Cadena
Joileen Richards
Gonzalo Cruz
Elizabeth Grajales
Julia Regul
Tali Djerassi
Carolina Cristancho
Beverlee Jean-Baptiste
Andrej Marjanovic
Sandra M. Hiari
Shirish Joshi
Lindsey Langenburg
Fernando Montejo
Kylie Murphy
Mariana Rodriguez Orte
Sarah Reinhard
JenJoy Roybal
Tisha Vaska

Leah Camille Dun
Stefano Galimberti
Lawrence M. Jacquette
Amy Sullivan
Alexa Helsell
Kent Ng
Andrea Barley
Yi Yen Zhang
Daniel Jinhwan
Susan Delamare
Shinya Trarsuji
Olta Molla
Eli Goteiner
Mary Doumas
Rodolfo Leyton
Otto Farquharson
Kok Chee Lee

ADVISORY BOARD

Bhavnani, Ashok – Architect
Bhavnani Studio, NYC

Bee, Carmi – Professor Emeritus
The City College of New York
RKT&B Architects & Planners

Bobenhausen, William – President
Sustainable Design Collaborative

Brown, Lance Jay – Professor
Final Year Design Coordinator
Bernard and Anne Spitzer School of Architecture
The City College of New York

Chen, Yuien – Executive Director
Harlem Sugar Hill Landmarks and Historic Districts

Feigenberg, Alan – Professor
Bernard and Anne Spitzer School of Architecture
The City College of New York

Henry, LaQuita – Project Manager
Heritage Health and Housing

McNeil, Garrison – Professor Emeritus
The City College of New York
Garrison McNeil & Associates Architects

O'Neal, Terrence – Architect
President, AIA National
Terrence O'Neal Architects

Reddick, John – Associate Vice-President
Education and Programming
Central Park Conservancy

Schiffman, Ron – Professor Emeritus
Pratt Center for Community Development

Sorkin, Michael – Professor
Director Urban Design Program
Bernard and Anne Spitzer School of Architecture
The City College of New York

Witherspoon, Karen – Director
Office of Urban & Governmental Affairs
The City College of New York

Hall, Camille – Director of Finance and Administration
Bernard and Anne Spitzer School of Architecture

PHOTO CREDITS

Introductory, closing and back cover photos: Rodolfo Leyton
Photo pages 39, 53, 63, 73, 77, 97, 107, 119, 141: Rodolfo Leyton
Photo pages 45, 49, 67, 133, 155, 169, 191: CCAC staff
Photo page 87: Otto Farquharsan
Photo pages 201, 213: Mary Doumas
Photo page 219: Eli Goteiner
Changing Streetscapes project: Albert Vecerka of Esto, photographer

All other images by CCAC staff or partners

COVER CREDITS

Cover Image:
Midtown-West: Manhattan's Future (2003)
for the Newman Real Estate Institute, Baruch College/CUNY

CCNY/CCAC:
Project Director/Ideal Green Designer: Lance Jay Brown, FAIA
Participants: Laila Al Khayer, Vanburn Brookes, Ryan Clarke,
Ethan Cohen, Tony Carona, Charles Cross, Michael Dox,
Sungkee Min, Julia regul, Laura stella, Eduard Urcia,
Lee Weintraub, Davis Brody Bond, LLP: Max Bond with Roland Charpentier,
Anna Dietzsch, Will Paxson, LeAnn Shelton

BOOK CREDITS

Creative Direction by Belén Matos
Edited by Achva Benzinberg Stein
Production by Oscar Riera Ojeda
Copy Editing by Kit Maude
Cover Design by Leo Malinow
Cover image "Urban Green" 2003, Lance Jay Brown, FAIA, DPACSA

OSCAR RIERA OJEDA
PUBLISHERS

ISBN 978-988-16194-1-9
Published by Oscar Riera Ojeda Publishers Limited
Printed in China by Artron Art Center

Oscar Riera Ojeda Publishers Limited
Unit 6, 22/F.,
Far East Consortium Building,
121 Des Voeux Road Central, Hong Kong
T: +852-5311-1625

Production Offices | China
Suit 19, Shenyun Road,
Nanshan District, Shenzhen 518055
T:+86-182-0098-3774

www.oropublishers.com | www.oscarrieraojeda.com
oscar@oscarrieraojeda.com